# Introduction to

# Residential Draw Inspections

### prepared by

### Trinity Performance Improvement

**TRINITY**
Real Estate Solutions, Inc®

### Documentation and Training

Trinity Real Estate Solutions, Inc. and subsidiaries Trinity Loan Administration, Trinity Inspection Services, Trinity Field Services, and Trinity Appraisal Services is committed to continuously improving our training materials and documentation through our Performance Improvement team. Constructive feedback from our partners is welcomed. If you have any suggestions or comments, please send them to info@trinityonline.com.

# Trinity Real Estate Solutions

Trinity Real Estate Solutions is a national provider of construction lending services, specialty inspections, property preservation, consulting services and valuation analysis for residential, commercial and business properties. All of Trinity's products are designed to mitigate risk and provide onsite assessments of properties. By partnering with customers, Trinity is able to set the standard for exceptional service while providing industry-leading response times. As a national company, we have the resources and experience to handle projects of any size and in any location. Trinity's growth and continued success can be attributed to our understanding of each customer's need for accurate and on-time information.

Trinity is a unified company that serves customers in the banking, mortgage lending, insurance and credit card industries. In order to sufficiently meet our customers' needs, we operate as four companies:

Trinity Appraisal Services, LLC

- ▶ Our goal is to provide the industry with a uniquely targeted range of new construction and renovation appraisal products and services. We operate as a trusted advisor to our customer's management team by providing unbiased guidance on critical lending decisions.

Trinity Field Services, LLC

- ▶ Let Trinity be your eyes in the field for residential and commercial property site inspections. Our team of over 10,000 field representatives are specialists, and we have the resources and experience to handle inspections nationwide. We consistently set ourselves apart by providing an unparalleled level of service, prompt order processing and comprehensive risk management.

Trinity Inspection Services, LLC

- ▶ At Trinity, we focus on our customers and the needs of the real estate industry. We are pleased to offer a wide range of products and services for residential and commercial properties. Whether you need a Property Information Report, Budget Review or Draw inspection, we will deliver superior customer service, technology innovations and industry-leading turn times.

Trinity Loan Administration, LLC

- ▶ Our commitment to our customers' success is a key differentiator as we continue to provide the industry with a uniquely comprehensive range of back office loan administration services. Whether a builder review, collateral assessment, title reports, lien waivers or permit verification, Trinity will focus on the administrative tasks of originating new construction or renovation loans so our customers can focus on their core business.

If you seek more information on our services you can visit www.trinityonline.com, call 888-573-8025 or email questions to info@trinityonline.com.

# Contents

INTRODUCTION.............................................................................v

    Welcome...............................................................................v

    Course Objectives................................................................v

    Target Audience..................................................................v

    Prerequisite Skills..............................................................vi

    Course Overview................................................................vii

MODULE 1: COURSE OVERVIEW...............................................1

    Module Objectives...............................................................1

    Introduction to Draw Inspections.........................................1

    What is a Draw Inspection?.................................................2

    The General Stages of Home Construction............................3

MODULE 2: SITE PREPARATION

    Module Objectives...............................................................4

    Definition of Site Preparation...............................................4

    Components of Site Preparation...........................................4

    Site Verification..................................................................5

    Demolition..........................................................................6

    Clearing.............................................................................7

    Stakeout............................................................................8

    Excavation.........................................................................9

    Rough Grading..................................................................10

    Temporary Barriers...........................................................10

    Retaining Walls.................................................................11

    Private Septic System........................................................12

Domestic Water Well.......................................................................................14

Pump House and Pressure Water.................................................................15

Module Review.............................................................................................16

**MODULE 3: FOUNDATION**

Module Objectives.......................................................................................17

Definition of Foundation..............................................................................17

Components of Site Preparation..................................................................17

Embedded Hardware...................................................................................18

Ground Utilities...........................................................................................19

      *Ground Plumbing*..................................................................................19

      *Ground Mechanical*..............................................................................19

      *Ground Electrical*.................................................................................20

Foundation..................................................................................................20

      *Pier and Beam*.....................................................................................20

      *Basement*............................................................................................22

      *Concrete Slab*......................................................................................23

Foundation and Retaining Walls.................................................................24

Weatherproofing.........................................................................................24

Module Review............................................................................................25

**MODULE 4: BUILDING ROUGH-IN**

Module Objectives.......................................................................................26

Definition of Building Rough-In....................................................................26

Components of Building Rough-In................................................................26

Rough Framing............................................................................................28

      *Structural Masonry*..............................................................................28

      *Structural Steel*....................................................................................29

      *Rough Framing Materials*.....................................................................30

Rough Framing / Carpentry.................................................................30

Interior Partitions...........................................................................32

Manufactured Trusses / Components.................................................33

Sheathing....................................................................................34

Lightweight Concrete Interior...........................................................35

**Rough Mechanicals.........................................................................36**

Plumbing Top-out..........................................................................36

Rough HVAC.................................................................................37

Rough Electrical.............................................................................39

Fire Protection..............................................................................40

Fire Place....................................................................................41

Security and Communications Pre-Wire..............................................41

**Modular / Prefabricated Housing.......................................................42**

Modular / Sectional Manufactured Home.............................................42

Package / Kit Home........................................................................43

**Module Review.............................................................................44**

**MODULE 5: EXTERIOR WEATHER-TIGHT................................................45**

**Module Objectives.........................................................................45**

**Definition of Exterior Weather-Tight..................................................45**

**Components of Site Preparation........................................................45**

**Roof Covering..............................................................................47**

**Waterproofing..............................................................................49**

**Windows....................................................................................50**

**Doors.......................................................................................51**

**Skylights...................................................................................52**

**Glazing.....................................................................................53**

**Soffit and Fascia..........................................................................53**

**Exterior Veneer**......................................................................**54**

*Siding*...............................................................................54

*Stucco*..............................................................................55

*Masonry Veneer*.................................................................56

**Exterior Trim**.........................................................................**58**

**Gutters/Downspouts**...............................................................**60**

**Garage Doors**.........................................................................**60**

**Ornamental Iron**....................................................................**61**

**Exterior Paint**.......................................................................**62**

**Rock Work**............................................................................**62**

**Module Review**.......................................................................**63**

**MODULE 6: INTERIOR FINISH**

**Module Objectives**...................................................................**64**

**Definition of Interior Finish**....................................................**64**

**Components of Site Preparation**................................................**64**

**Insulation**............................................................................**65**

**Drywall (Plaster)**...................................................................**67**

**Cabinetry**.............................................................................**68**

**Finish Materials and Millwork**..................................................**69**

**Interior Stairs**.......................................................................**70**

**Interior Doors**.......................................................................**71**

**Module Review**.......................................................................**72**

**MODULE 7: FINISH ITEMS**.........................................................**73**

**Module Objectives**...................................................................**73**

**Definition of Finish Items**........................................................**73**

**Components of Site Preparation**................................................**73**

**Countertops**..........................................................................**75**

Tub/Shower/Enclosures.................................................................76

Interior Paint.............................................................................77

Hard Surface Finish Flooring........................................................78

Carpeting..................................................................................81

Appliances.................................................................................82

Finish Hardware..........................................................................83

Finish Plumbing...........................................................................84

Plumbing Fixtures........................................................................85

Finish Electrical..........................................................................87

Lighting Fixtures.........................................................................87

Finish Heating, Ventilation, A/C....................................................88

Bath Accessories.........................................................................89

Tub and Shower Doors/Mirrors......................................................90

Finish Grading.............................................................................91

Pool/Spa....................................................................................91

Hardscape..................................................................................93

Fencing Including Gates................................................................94

Landscaping...............................................................................95

Central Vacuum..........................................................................96

Module Review............................................................................97

MODULE 8: DRAW FORM.................................................................98

Module Objectives........................................................................98

Understanding Various Types of Draw Inspection Forms.....................98

General Components of a Draw Inspection Form................................98

Report Line Items.......................................................................101

Photo Section............................................................................102

INDEX.........................................................................................103

# Introduction

## Welcome

This course contains basic information about draw inspections.

## Course Objectives

After completing this course, you will be able to:

► Identify the six basic stages of home construction

► Describe the components of each of the six stages of home construction

► Estimate the percentage of stage completion based on evidence given

► Explain the draw inspection process

► Define the different types of draw inspection forms

► Identify all the components of a draw inspection form

► Complete a draw inspection report

## Target Audience

Anyone with an interest in the basics of draw inspection services as well as new and renovation construction lending can benefit from the material in this course.

## Prerequisite Skills

None.

# Course Overview

This course has eight modules, which include objectives and review questions.

| Module | Title |
|--------|-------|
| 1 | Course Overview |
| 2 | Site Preparation |
| 3 | Foundation |
| 4 | Building Rough-In |
| 5 | Exterior Weather-Tight |
| 6 | Interior Finish |
| 7 | Finish Items |
| 8 | Draw Form |

This course may be used as a self-study guide.

# Module #1
# Course Overview

**Course Objectives** — After completing this module, you will be able to:

☐ Identify the six basic stages of home construction

☐ Describe the components of each of the six stages of home construction

☐ Estimate the percentage of stage completion based on evidence given

☐ Explain the draw inspection process

This course is designed to familiarize draw inspectors with the general stages of home construction. Because each stage of construction consists of several steps, it is important for an inspector to recognize each step in order to make accurate estimates.

Estimating the amount of a project that has been completed contains both **objective** and **subjective** elements. The information in this course is intended to give you **objective** starting points for your estimates. Although these starting points can be used as guidelines, the individual nature of each construction project requires you to use your experience and sound judgment when making your estimates.

Home construction techniques vary across the different regions of the United States. For example, in some regions it is common for a home to have a basement, while in other regions, basements are not available. Because of these variations, not all aspects of construction can be discussed in this course. It is important for you to become familiar with any additional information that may be specific to your area, but is not mentioned in this course.

In addition to variations in the types of structures built, the timing of some construction steps can differ. For example, a private septic tank may be added at the beginning of the construction project, or it may be installed at or after the midway point in construction. For consistency, these items will be mentioned in the stage of construction where they could first occur and this course will point out in which other stages of construction they could occur.

## What is a Draw Inspection?

Construction Draw Inspections are inspections for modular and manufactured housing, remodels and conventional new residential designs.

A draw inspection is a visible observation of progress of a construction project. It may also be referred to as a "progress inspection."

The draw inspection is the result of a builder/contractor requesting to be paid by a bank/mortgage company or owner for the work finished on a construction project.

The term "draw" refers to the money paid to the builder/contractor for work completed that is "drawn" from the loan amount a borrower or business has been approved for the construction project and is available to pay for completed construction.

A draw inspection report includes a listing of the items for construction (foundation, framing, roof, electrical, plumbing, cabinets, etc.) and the associated cost for each item. Hard and soft costs will appear on the report. Hard costs are the obvious parts of construction that can be pictured. Soft costs are all costs that are not directly related to physical construction such as the builders reserve, architect, permits or profit. Basically, a soft cost is anything that cannot be pictured. A field representative (draw inspector) visits the construction site and submits an opinion of the percent of completion for an item. The field rep also provides photos as evidence of the construction progress. Draw inspectors may visit the construction site frequently depending on how many draw requests a construction project requires.

The purpose of a draw inspection is to ensure money is only paid to the builder/contractor for the work completed. This process reduces lender risk of providing money for work not completed, known as over funding, by providing an assessment of a project at a specific point in time.

A draw inspection does not assess or determine quality, consistency within plan (blue print) specifications, governmental requirements (permits, city inspectors) or matters related to changes to the scope of the project. The report is intended to inform the lender how much of the physical work is visibly completed in order to assist in their internal disbursement decisions.

There are no official state, national or international certifications or licensing requirements to perform a draw inspection. Typically a draw inspector has experience with construction and may also be a "home inspector," property appraiser, construction specialist or real estate agent.

Banks/mortgage lenders may either contract directly with a draw inspector or work with a vendor management company who handles fulfillment of the inspection and report. The advantage of using a vendor management company is the additional insurance coverage, centralized scheduling and order tracking, web site, standard communication, technology (including integration with a bank/lender's loans processing system) and centralized quality control process.

## The General Stages of Home Construction

For the purpose of this course, construction is broken down into six stages or phases of construction.

- ➤ Site Preparation
- ➤ Foundation
- ➤ Building Rough-In
- ➤ Exterior Weather-Tight
- ➤ Interior Finish
- ➤ Finish Items

Each stage is represented by a module in this manual. Each module contains objectives that you will be able to accomplish, definitions relevant to the stage and photographs that show the various steps of completion for each stage. At the end of each module, you will find review questions designed to help you internalize the material presented.

# Module #2
# Site Preparation

**Objectives** — After completing this module you will be able to:

☐ Describe the components within the Site Preparation Stage
☐ Estimate completion based on photo evidence

**Definition** — Site preparation is the process of making the property ready for construction to begin. Site preparation consists of several components, each representing specific activities to be performed during construction. Estimates should accurately reflect the amount of completed work.

## Components of Site Preparation

- **Site Verification:** Identifying the piece of property upon which the home will be built.

- **Demolition:** The destruction and removal of existing structures on the building site.

- **Clearing:** The mowing of grass and weeds, the removal of large rocks, and trimming and removal of trees and shrubs.

- **Stakeout:** The outlining of the structure perimeter with wooden stakes.

- **Excavation:** The removal of soil during rough grading.

- **Grading (Rough Grading):** The compaction and leveling of soil for buildings and driveways.

- **Temporary Barrier:** Bracing to prevent caving in of excavated soil.

- **Retaining Walls:** Holds back a slope and prevents soil erosion primarily used in areas with uneven ground.

- **Private Septic System:** A concrete or fiberglass waste water container buried below the house grade.

- **Domestic Water Well:** The water source for homes not connected to any city utilities.

- **Pump House and Pressure Water:** Water reservoir positioned between the well and the house.

## Site Verification

Prior to making any estimation, **it is vital** that you verify you are at the correct property. No inspection may continue without site verification. You can verify the site using the following methods:

✓ Plat map or prior photos of property
✓ Addresses posted on the property or on the house
✓ Permits identifying the property
✓ Meet the owner/builder at the property

*Photos of the Property*

Mailboxes and curb signs are excellent ways to validate a property address.

*Addresses posted on the Property or the House*

Many construction projects may have the address painted on the house or dumpster for ease of identification.

*Permits Identifying the Property*

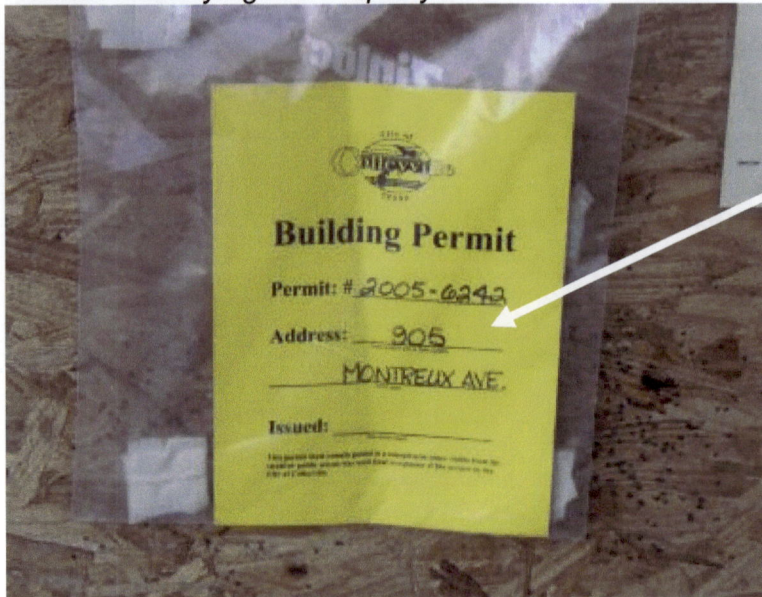

Most cities require permits to be posted in a highly visible location during construction.

## Demolition

Before new construction can begin, any old structures not being retained must be torn down and removed.

*Demolition in process*

This photo shows demolition underway but not complete.

Demolition can include removing entire structures or just portions of the structure ranging from the roof to interior walls.

## Clearing

Clearing the area is the next step in the preparation of the site. This includes the mowing of grass and weeds, the removal of large rocks and the trimming and removal of trees and shrubs.

*Clearing in process.*

This photo shows clearing at 50% because cut tress and shrubs remain in the property.

*Rock Removal in process*

This photo shows that the rocks have been marked for removal. However, until they are removed the process of clearing would still be estimated at 0%.

*Completed Clearing*

All shrubs, trees, grass and weeds have been cut and removed. This property would be considered 100% cleared.

## Stakeout

Staking out the property defines the borders of the area to be built upon.

*Staked Out*

Stakes are clearly visible in this photo.

## Excavation

Excavation is the removal of soil during rough grading.

*Multi-layered Excavation*

Excavated areas

This photo shows the areas where soil has been removed.

*Another Excavated Site*

The excavation at this sites is 100% complete.

## Rough grading

Rough grading is the compacting and leveling of the soil in preparation of buildings and driveways.

*Rough Grading*

This rough grading is 100% complete.

## Temporary Barriers

On some sites, Temporary Barriers may be necessary and are designed to be removed after construction. *Silt Fences* and *Shoring* are typical types of temporary bracing or barriers used to prevent excavated soil from caving in.

*Temporary Barrier*

Silt fences are used primarily to control erosion since the soil has been disturbed and is now loose.

*Shoring*

Shoring is usually constructed of plywood and will be removed after the installation of the permanent structure.

## Retaining Walls

Retaining walls hold back a slope and prevent soil erosion used primarily in areas with uneven ground.

*Retaining Walls*

The best way to estimate a retaining wall is to gauge how much more construction of the wall remains if any.

This photo appears 100%, because no other work appears needed.

## Private Septic System

A private septic system is a waste water container buried below the house grade. It is required when a home is not connected to city utilities.

A septic system can be added to the property anytime during the construction process so it's important to know what's on the draw inspection.

This septic system is in the early stages of installation. Tank and pipes to leach field are visible.

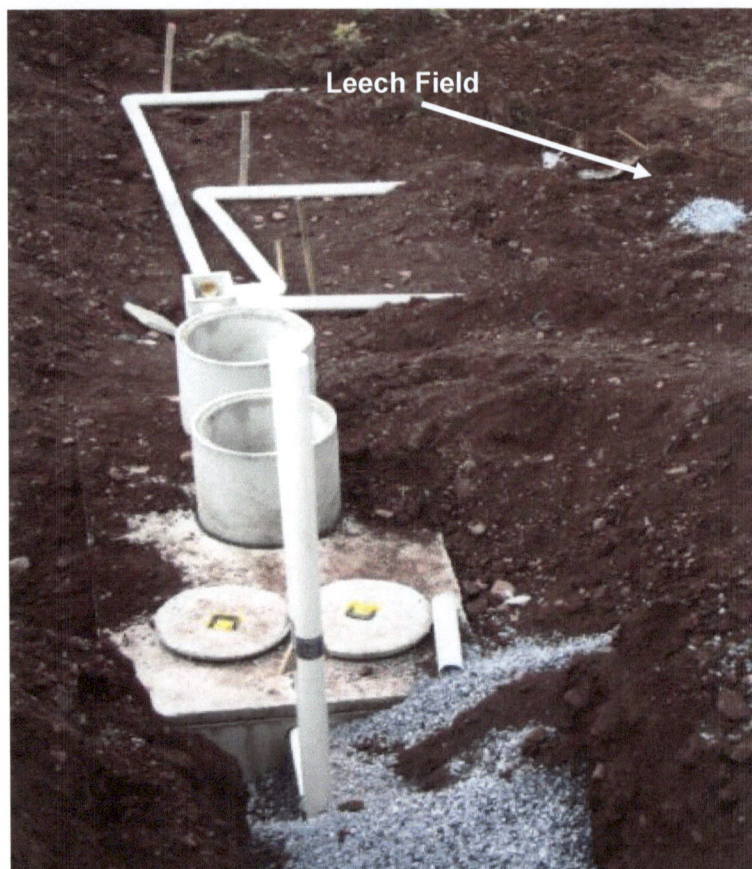

This system is 95% complete. The leach field needs to be covered and lids placed on tank.

*Fully installed Septic Tank*

This system is 100% complete.

*Identifying a Septic Installation*

When looking for a septic system, do not assume it is installed due to finish grading or disturbed soil. If it is not visible (tank covers), other measures of verifying are needed. Using only the photo on the left, the septic is 0%.

Another verification method is a city or county septic inspection certificate. Most city or county jurisdictions require a septic system to be certified and inspected by a licensed inspector.

## Domestic Water Well

A domestic water well is the water source for homes not connected to any city utilities. Domestic water wells are usually only visible by their well heads.

*Well Head*

*Well Head*

*Drill Truck*

When the well is still in the process of being drilled, it should be considered 50% complete.

## Pump House and Pressure Water

As part of the well system, the pump and tank are positioned between the well head and the homes interior water lines.

*Pressure Tank*

Pressure Tank

**Review**

1. What methods can you use to verify that you are looking at the correct property?

   _____

   _____

   _____

2. What is typically removed during the clearing process?

   _____

   _____

   _____

3. Name the process of leveling and compacting soil to prepare for buildings and driveways. _____

4. What kinds of structures are used to prevent excavated soil from caving in?

   _____

# Module #3
# Foundation

**Objectives** — After completing this module you will be able to:

☐ Identify the various types of foundations
☐ Understand how foundation systems vary across the country
☐ Estimate completion based on photo evidence

## Definition

This phase of the construction project includes the foundation and all work required to be completed beneath or within the foundation base. There are two basic components that need to be completed prior to the foundation construction: underground utilities and embedded hardware. The foundation is the supporting or load-bearing portion of a structure below the first floor construction, also known as "below grade."

## Components of Foundation

- **Embedded Hardware:** Wall tie down bolts, fasteners and/or brackets securing the house to the foundation.

- **Ground Utilities/Mechanicals**: All mechanicals (water, sewer, electrical conduit) installed beneath grade level (slab or basement) and connections to public utilities.

- **Foundation Types**: The foundation is the supporting or load-bearing portion of a structure below the first floor construction, also known as "below grade."
    - Pier & Beam
    - Basement
    - Concrete Slab

- **Foundation – Retaining Walls:** Retaining walls incorporated into the house if constructed on an incline.

- **Weatherproofing:** Use of black tar-like substance that prevents moisture from entering the structure and is installed below grade on the foundation.

## Embedded Hardware

Embedded hardware includes: wall tie-down bolts, fasteners and brackets that secure the house to the foundation. These items are added to the foundation while the concrete is in a liquid state. As the concrete hardens, the hardware is secured into place.

*Wall Tie-down Bolts*

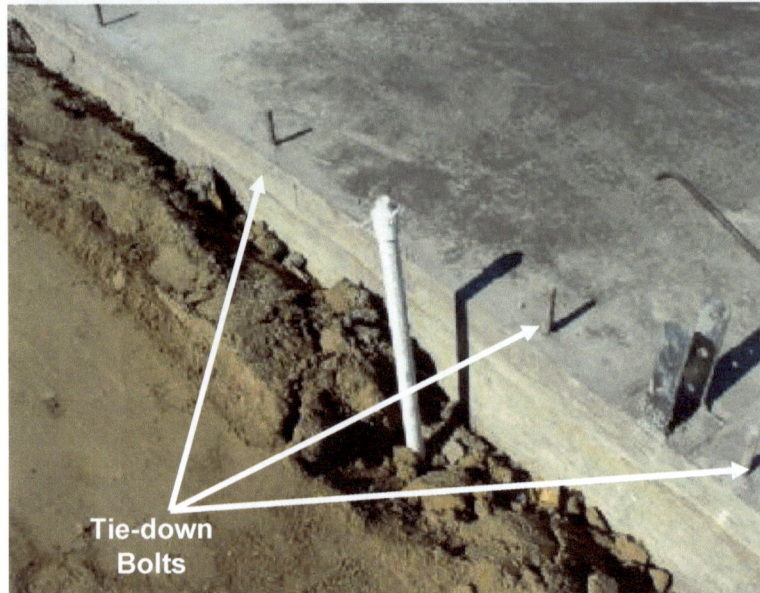

Tie-down bolts are used to attach lumber flush with the foundation.

At this stage you should consider a foundation 100% complete.

*Fasteners*

Fasteners are used primarily to attach vertical lumber to the foundation elements.

## Ground Utilities

All utilities installed beneath grade level (slab or basement) and connections to public utilities. These include Ground Plumbing, Mechanicals and Electrical.

## Ground Plumbing

Ground plumbing is complete when all underground plumbing pipes are installed and connected to the public utilities.

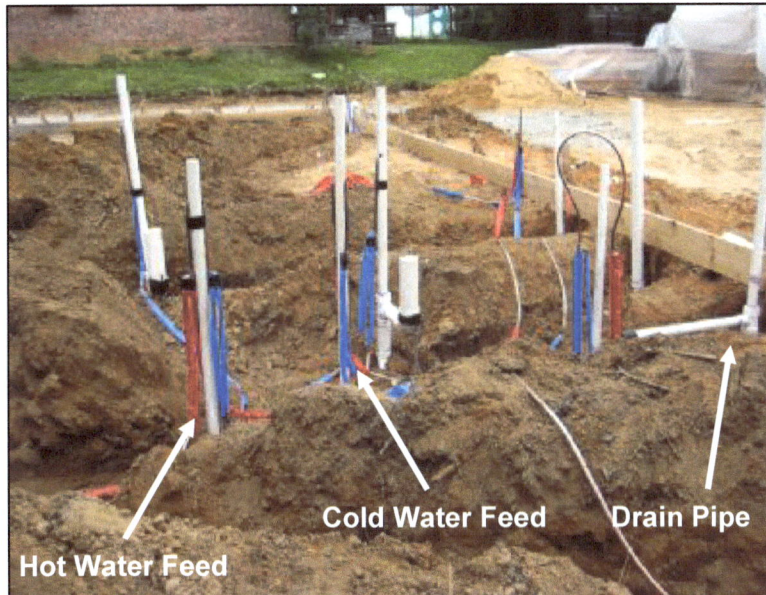

This photo shows ground plumbing after trenching. The Red and Blue colors indicate Hot and Cold feeds and the white (or black) PVC piping indicates a drain exiting the house.

## Ground Mechanical

Ground mechanical consists of underground utility connections and/or HVAC venting through the foundation.

This photo shows ground utility connections running to the edge of the property.

## Ground Electrical

Ground electrical is complete when the electrical power from the municipality is brought to the house under the ground.

The photo on the left depicts ground electrical protruding through a poured slab foundation. It is probably going to connect to a manifold to be distributed throughout the house.

## Foundation

The foundation is the supporting portion of a structure below the first floor construction capable of bearing the entire weight of the house.

There are three basic types of foundation systems:
- ✓ Pier and Beam
- ✓ Basement (Poured, cinder block)
- ✓ Concrete Slab (Rebar, Post-tension)

### Pier and Beam

Pier and beam foundations are used to raise the first floor level above the surrounding area. Most pier and beam foundations leave a "crawl space" of approximately 1 to 3 feet between the ground and the bottom of the first floor. Pier and beam foundations consist of two elements: piers and footers. Piers are usually 8" or 10" thick concrete pads or columns installed to support the first floor joists. Footers are the poured concrete walls (generally 6" to 8" wide) buried in the ground used to support the perimeter of the structure. Beams are wooden floor joists, usually 2" X 12" lumber, that are set in the fasteners and are generally laid in place in pairs.

*Piers*

This photo shows the piers with fasteners embedded but without the support beams installed.

Note - The foundation contractor does not install the beams. Beams are installed by the framing contractor.

A good thing to remember:
Piers – vertical support
Footers – horizontal support

*Footers*

This photo shows the footers with structural steel protruding from the top. A cinder block wall will be placed on top of the footers with the steel anchoring the two together.

The term footers and piers are commonly interchanged.

Piers are mainly used in depth stabilization/support and footers are support pads/base.

## Basement
Basements provide structural support for the house while increasing the usable space within a house. There are two basic types of basement construction: poured concrete and cinder block construction.

*Poured Concrete*

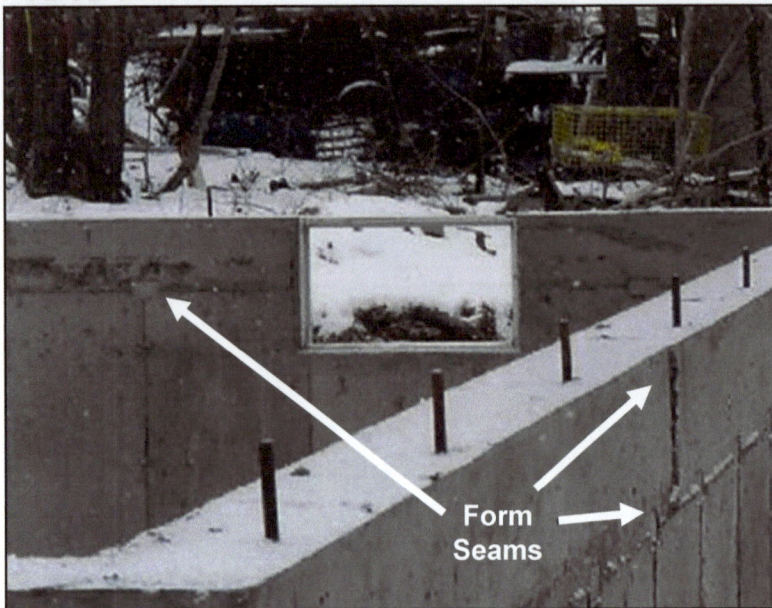

This photo shows the seams from the concrete forms as well as embedded hardware sticking out of the top.

*Cinder Block Wall*

## Concrete Slab

A concrete slab foundation is concrete poured directly above the ground and can be either a post-tension slab or a rebar slab. Rebar slab foundations include steel rebar reinforcement providing extra strength.

*Rebar Slab*

This foundation would be considered approximately 40% complete. There is no concrete poured.

## Post Tension Slab

Post Tension slabs have embedded tension rods that allow for realignment and tightening over time. Post tension rods allow the foundation to be adjusted as the house settles with the soil.

*Post Tension Slab*

As houses age, the surrounding soil moves and may cause the foundation to move and potentially crack. The rods can be tightened to pull the slab together minimizing cracks.

## Foundation – Retaining Walls

Some foundations can incorporate retaining walls in the event the house is constructed on an incline. Not only will the foundation support the weight of the structure but it will also prevent the soil erosion from around the house.

*Foundation – Retaining Walls*

These are most common in split-level homes constructed on hillsides.

## Weatherproofing

Weatherproofing is a black tar-like substance developed to prevent moisture from entering the structure and is installed below grade on the foundation.

*Weatherproofing*

Weatherproofing should begin at the bottom of the foundation and run to approximately 6" above the ground line for the best protection.

**Review**

1. What are the three main foundation types?

   _____

   _____

   _____

2. What is the difference between a footer and a pier in construction?

   _____

   _____

   _____

3. What are the two types of slab foundations?

   _____

   _____

4. Where should weather-proofing be applied?

   _____

# Module #4
# Building Rough-In

**Objectives** — After completing this module you will be able to:

- ☐ Identify the various components involved with Building Rough-In
- ☐ Identify different types of exterior framing techniques and building materials
- ☐ Understand the different types of construction materials used in framing
- ☐ Estimate completion based on photo evidence

## Definition

This phase of the construction project includes all rough framing, rough mechanical and any modular or prefabricated work on a house.

## Components of Building Rough-In

- **Rough Framing:** All activities and work in completing the load bearing exterior and interior walls of a construction project. The most common materials used in the United States are wood, concrete and steel. The following list includes items typically included in rough framing:
    - o Structural Masonry
    - o Structural Steel
    - o Rough Framing Materials
    - o Rough Framing / Carpentry
    - o Interior Partitions
    - o Manufactured Trusses / Components
    - o Sheathing
    - o Lightweight Concrete Interior
- **Rough Mechanicals**: The installation of plumbing, HVAC, electric and any other utilities that will be hidden from view when the house is complete.
    - o Rough Plumbing/Plumbing Top-Out
    - o Rough HVAC
    - o Rough Electrical

- o Fire Protection
- o Security and Communications Pre-wire
- **Modular / Prefabricated Housing**: Housing primarily constructed offsite and shipped to the site ready to assemble.
  - o Modular / Section Housing
  - o Package Kit Home

## Rough Framing

Rough framing includes all activities associated with the completion of the load bearing exterior and interior walls of a construction project. The most common materials used in the United States are wood, concrete and steel.

### Structural Masonry

Structural framing support for the house generally made of concrete-type products most commonly used in exterior walls.

*Cinder Block Exterior Construction*

Cinder block exterior wall construction is most common in Florida and is primarily used for hurricane protection.

The last step in the external cinderblock wall is the tie beam. In this type of construction, a tie beam is placed at the top of the walls with a form that holds poured concrete, making a band around the top of the walls that holds the walls together.

*Poured Concrete Exterior Wall Construction*

Poured concrete walls are becoming more common for exterior wall framing construction.

## Structural Steel

Structural steel is the support for the floor decking. It can be found in houses with a basement but can also be used to support all floors in multi-story houses.

*Structural Steel*

In the picture on the left, Structural Steel would be considered 100% complete.

Structural steel usage can vary from site to site. If unsure about how much structural steel will be used in a project, consult the cost breakdown or blueprints or discuss with the lender or borrower.

## Rough Framing Materials

Materials used in the construction of the frame of the house including the exterior sheathing and roof decking. Materials generally used are lumber, steel, concrete and cinder block, and foam board.

*Materials dropped and covered*

Framing materials are usually dropped off at the work site in bulk still in weatherproof wrap.

## Rough Framing / Carpentry

Rough Framing is the labor to assemble lumber, foam board, structural masonry or steel used for the structural members of a building such as studs, joists and rafters.

*Stick-built construction*

The picture to the left shows a "stick-built" construction, meaning the house is built from individual pieces of 2"X4" or 2"X6" lumber.

Steel framing is another type of interior frame product.

## Steel Framed Construction

**Steel Studs**

The picture to the left shows steel framing built from 2" X 4" or 2" X 6" steel material.

## Completed Rough Framing

**Moisture barrier**

At this point, the house is referred to as "Closed in." The moisture barrier is applied once the sheathing is installed.

Sheathing is defined on page 34.

*Interior Stair Framing*

Stairs are 0% Complete

The picture on the left depicts the roughed-in stairs. At this point in construction, stairs are considered 0% complete since the finish out of the stairs is completed by a separate subcontractor.

## Interior Partitions

Interior Partitions are the interior walls usually constructed of 2" X 4" or 2" X 6'" lumber.

*Interior Partitions*

Interior partitions also support a portion of the weight of the house as well as providing structural support for the attic rafters or second floor decking.

## Manufactured Trusses / Components

Trusses (wood or steel) support connecting the roof to the exterior walls

*Trusses*

Interior partitions also support a portion of the weight of the house as well as providing structural support for the attic rafters or second floor decking.

*Manufactured Trusses*

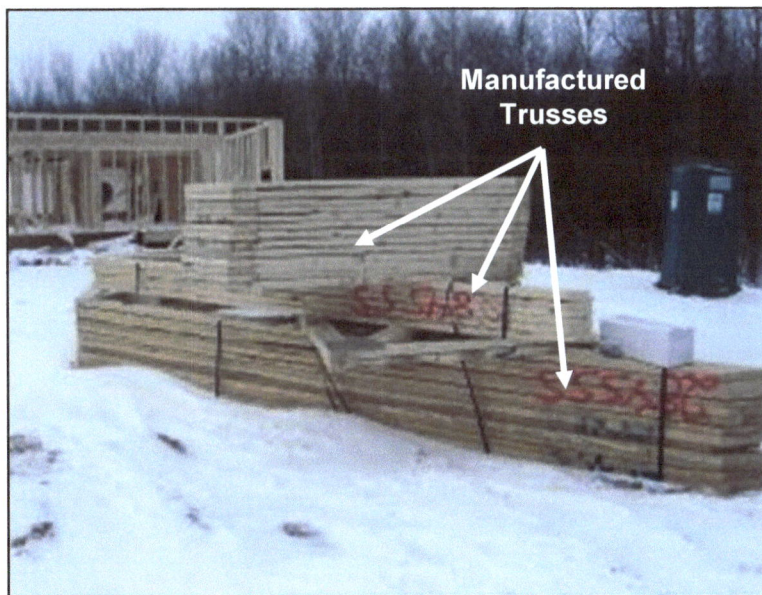

Trusses are commonly manufactured offsite and shipped to the worksite ready to install.

## Sheathing

Sheathing is the plywood or foam covering of the exterior walls on a house. It may sometimes include the roof decking or sheathing as well.

*Exterior Wall Sheathing*

**Plywood Sheathing**

Sheathing is generally constructed from plywood or Oriented Strand Board ("OSB"). OSB is a plywood-like material composed of small chips of wood pressed and glued together.

*Foam Board*

**Foam Board**

Foam board is often used for non-load bearing portions of the exterior sheathing to save on costs.

## Roof Decking

Roof decking or sheathing consists of the plywood sheets installed on top of the trusses (also called rafters) to provide support for the shingles or roof tiles.

## Lightweight Concrete Interior

Lightweight interior concrete is poured concrete not designed to support the weight of the house.

*Concrete ready to pour*

Lightweight interior concrete is most commonly found in garages, patios and porches but can include driveways and walkways if they are not specified elsewhere in the cost breakdown.

## Rough Mechanicals

Rough Mechanicals includes the installation of plumbing, HVAC, electric and any other utilities that will be hidden from view when the house is complete.

### Plumbing Top-out

Rough plumbing that includes piping coming up from the ground or basement through the walls and vented out the top of the house. Other common terms for this are $2^{nd}$ plumbing, plumbing (tub-set), and also rough plumbing if there is no need for plumbing in pre-foundation work.

*Plumbing Top-out*

Copper tubing (sometimes insulated) provides water to plumbing fixtures. PVC piping (usually black or white) drains waste water from the house to the sewer or septic system..

*Plumbing Top-out (Vent Stacks)*

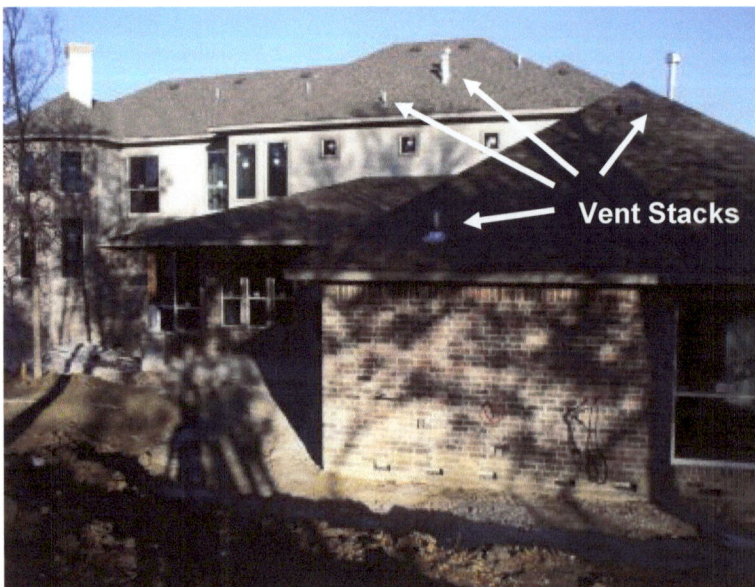

Vent stacks sticking out of the roof indicate plumbing top-out is 100% complete.

## Rough HVAC

Rough Heating, Ventilation and Air Conditioning (HVAC) includes the round or rectangular metal pipes or tubing installed for distributing warm (or cold) air from the furnace to rooms in the home.

*Ductwork*

Ductwork is the insulated tubing that directs the air flow to all interior areas. These tubes run in the attic, basements and in the framing concealed behind the finished out walls.

*Furnace and Ductwork*

The furnace designated for basements can be installed at any time. Other types of furnaces require installation before the attic is closed off.

## Boiler

Boiler

Sometimes the ductwork is run from a boiler rather than from the furnace. This practice is more common in the Northeast and Midwest.

## Radiant Heat

Radiant heat flooring has tubes running under the finished floor material.

## Rough Electrical

All wiring, outlet and fixture boxes, and the outside panel box are installed (before insulation and drywall).

*Electrical Boxes at Rough-In*

Switch and Outlet Boxes

Switches and outlets that are installed in the plug and switch boxes are not part of rough electric. Switches, outlets and switch plates are part of Finish Electrical.

*Fixture Boxes Roughed In*

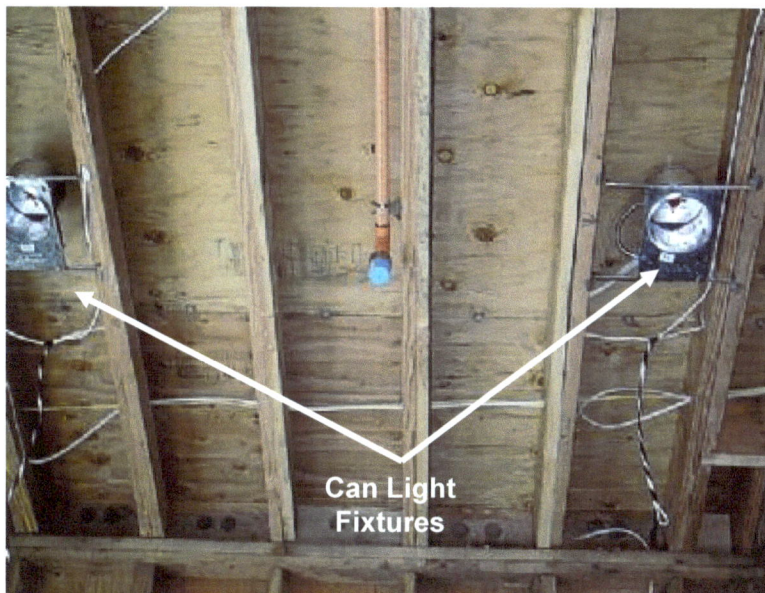

Can Light Fixtures

Most light fixture boxes must be installed prior to insulation and drywall.

*Panel Box and Wires*

The panel box is the primary juncture for the house's wiring to tie into the city utilities.

## Fire Protection

Plumbing and sprinkler head are installed for fire suppression throughout the house.

*Sprinkler Piping*

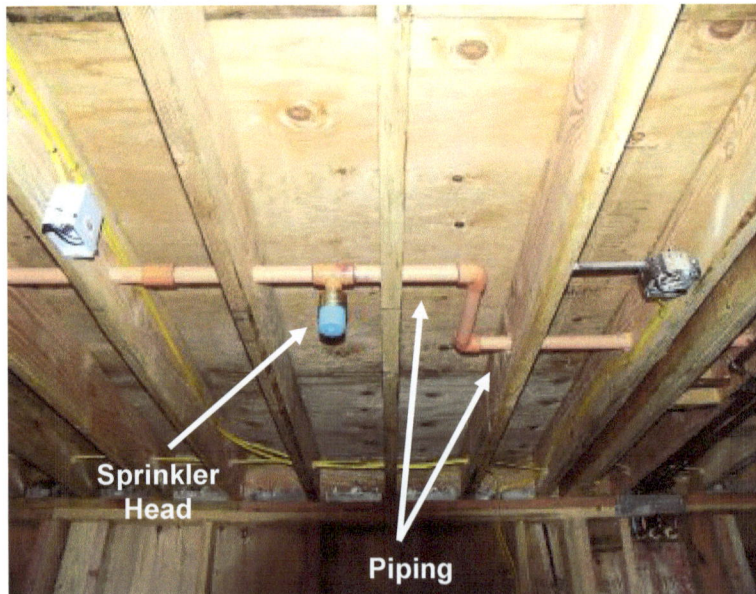

Sprinkler systems are most common in California but are increasing in numbers throughout the rest of the country, especially in large homes.

## Fireplace

The firebox and flue extended to the exterior of the house are installed in this step.

*Firebox and Flue*

The fireplace at the left is 100% complete.

## Security & Communications Pre-wire

Pre-wiring can include security systems, communication, intercom and sound systems within the house.

*Coaxial Cable Pre-wiring*

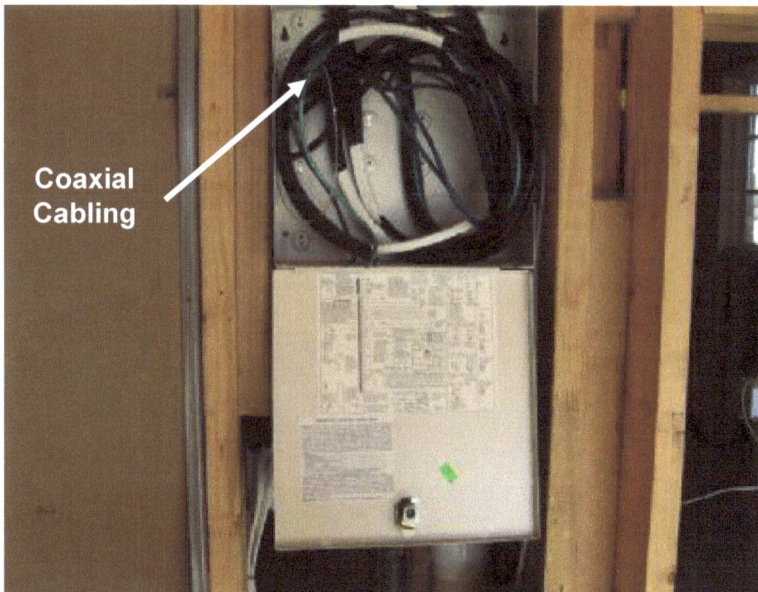

These are usually collected at one central point in the house. The collection point depends on the type of system.

## Modular / Sectional Manufactured Home

Another type of construction used extensively in the U.S. is modular or manufactured housing. A manufactured house is primarily constructed offsite and is shipped to the site ready to assemble. The assembly of a modular home usually only takes one day to complete and can even occur the day of delivery.

*Crane setting Modular Sections in Place-1*

The following two pictures show a crane setting a modular home in place.

*Crane setting Modular Sections in Place-2*

The modular section is set in place.

## Package / Kit Home

A package or kit home is a structure whose parts are designed to be assembled onsite in a very short timeframe. Log homes are considered packaged or kit homes.

*Log Home*

This log home is in the process of log stacking.

*Kit Home being delivered*

**Review**

1. What are three of the items that make up Rough Mechanicals?

   _____

   _____

   _____

2. Furnaces are generally found in the _____ or the

   _____.

3. Does Rough Electrical include the installation of the switch plates and plugs in the walls? _____

4. Lightweight interior concrete is generally poured with the foundation.  T / F

5. List the primary types of exterior framing materials most commonly used in the U.S.

   _____

   _____

   _____

6. During Rough Framing, interior stairs are considered _____ % complete.

# Module #5

# Exterior Weather-Tight

**Objectives** — After completing this module you will be able to:

- ☐ Identify all components to be completed during this stage of construction
- ☐ Estimate completion based on photo evidence

## Definition

Exterior Weather-Tight indicates that all products are installed to seal the house from the elements, preventing any moisture penetration into the home.

## Components of Exterior Weather-Tight

- **Roof Covering:** Roofing includes the installation of the felt paper which serves as a moisture barrier and the shingles or tiles which are for both weather protection and aesthetic purposes.
- **Waterproofing:** The installation of the shower pans and/or "mud." Underneath wet areas within the house.
- **Windows:** Windows are generally installed during framing to aid in the "Close-in" of the house. This prevents weather intrusion from damaging the interior wood or other materials inside the house during construction.
- **Doors:** Doors are also usually installed during framing to aid in the "Close-in" of the house. This prevents weather intrusion from damaging the interior wood or other materials inside the house during construction.
- **Skylights:** Fixed windows installed in the roof designed to allow natural light into the house.
- **Glazing:** Glazing means the panes of glass that are inserted into the window sash and frame. It can also mean thin plastic film applied to windows during construction to minimize breakage.
- **Soffit & Fascia**: The soffit is the underside of the eaves connecting the exterior walls to the roof and is usually made of wood, vinyl or composite products such as Hardy Board. The fascia is the siding that installs on the butt end of the rafters and is usually made of 1"X4" or 1"X6" lumber or composite products.

- **Exterior Veneer:** Finish product put on the home to serve as a barrier from weather but providing no structural support for the home.
  - o **Siding:** Exterior covering made of vinyl or aluminum installed to weatherproof the house.
  - o **Stucco:** Exterior covering made of durable plaster-like substance installed to weatherproof the house. It includes the wire mesh, coating and sealer but not paint.
  - o **Masonry Veneer:** Brick veneer on the exterior of a home to provide weather protection but not designed to support the weight of the structure.
- **Exterior Trim:** Exterior trim work originally intended as weatherproofing but today is primarily for decorative purposes.
- **Gutters/Downspouts**: Metal or vinyl gutters installed to carry water away from the structure.
- **Garage Doors:** Installation of garage doors, supports and openers.
- **Ornamental Iron:** Ironwork inside or outside of house not designed to support any structural weight.
- **Exterior Paint:** Latex or oil-base covering used primarily for weatherproofing but also decorative purposes.
- **Rock Work:** The removal of large rocks or boulders from the worksite.

## Roof Covering

Roofing includes the installation of the felt paper which serves as a moisture barrier and the shingles, tin or tiles that are for both weather protection and aesthetic purposes.

*Felt Paper*

The felt paper underlayment serves as a moisture barrier and is the first part of the roof to be installed.

The percent complete would be estimated to be roughly 15%. The cost of laying the felt paper is low relative to the cost of installing the shingles or tile.

*Shingled Roof*

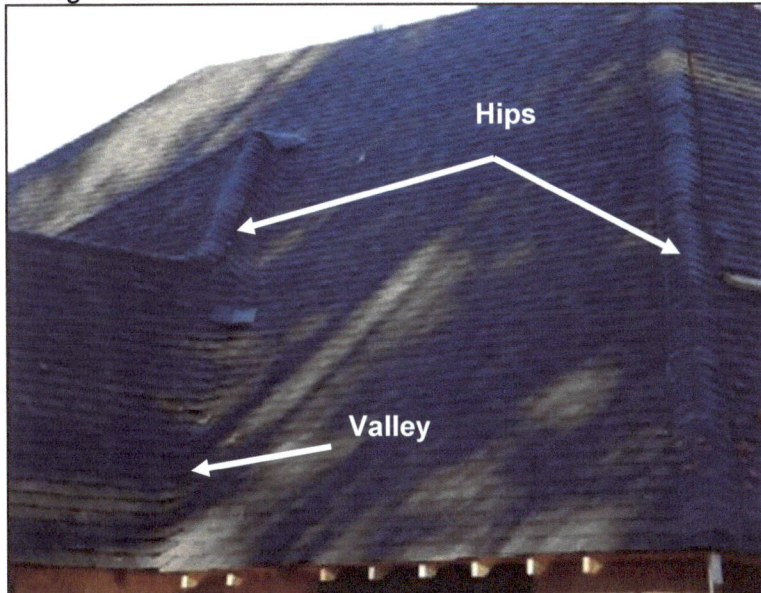

The picture at the left depicts a shingled roof.

## Tile Roof

Tiled roofs are most common in the southwestern part of the U.S.

## Tin Roof

*Stacked Roof*

**Tiles Stacked on Roof**

A stacked roof indicates the paper is down and the shingles or tiles are stacked on the roof but not permanently installed. This aids in the installation and reduces theft losses.

## Waterproofing

Waterproofing in this photo is the installation of the shower pans and/or "mud" underneath wet areas within the house.

*Shower Pan*

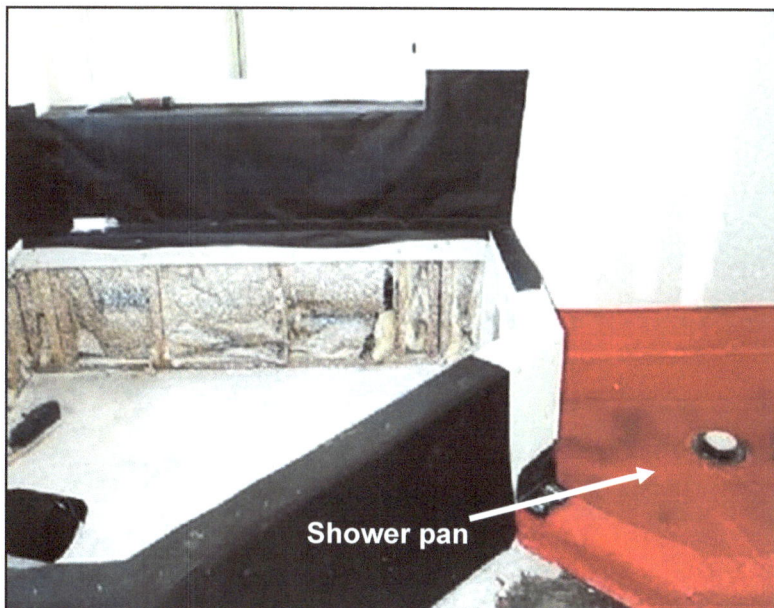

**Shower pan**

## Windows

Windows are generally installed during framing to aid in the "close-in" of the house. This prevents weather intrusion from damaging the interior wood or other materials inside the house during construction.

*Windows onsite, not installed*

Lenders have different policies regarding funding for materials onsite but not installed. The windows at the left are ready to install. Typically the lender is told materials are onsite but given 0% completion.

*Windows installed*

The windows on the left are 100% complete.

## Doors

Doors are also usually installed during framing to aid in the "close-in" of the house. This prevents weather intrusion from damaging the interior wood or other materials inside the house during construction.

*Exterior Doors installed*

*Temporary Front Door*

It is not uncommon for builders to install a temporary front door during construction since most entry doors are quite expensive and easily broken. All other exterior doors are installed during framing and the temporary door is usually replaced with the permanent one during finish out.

*Doors not installed*

Lenders have different policies regarding funding for materials onsite, but not installed. The entry door on the left is ready to install.

## Skylights

Skylights are fixed windows installed in the roof designed to allow natural light into the house.

*Skylights installed*

## Glazing

Window glazing means the panes of glass that are inserted into the window sash and frame.

*Glazing on Windows*

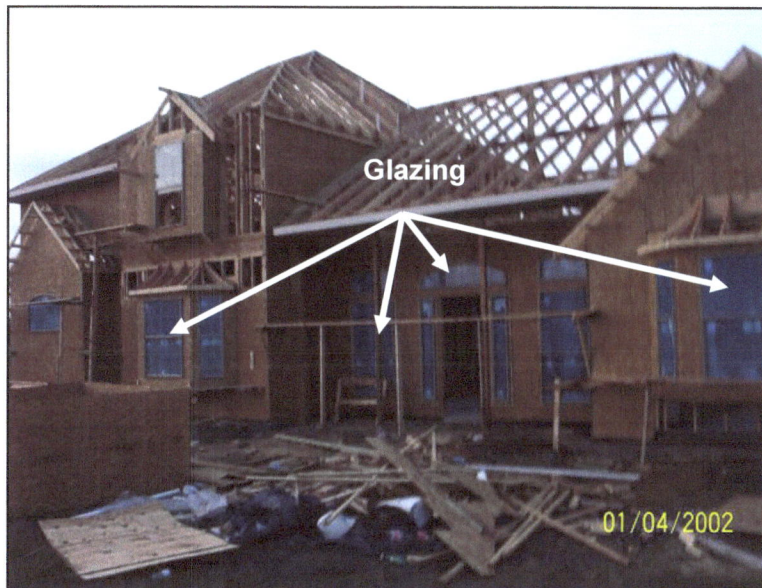

Gazing can also be a thin plastic film applied to windows during construction to minimize breakage during construction. Glazing is usually removed during final cleanup.

## Soffit & Fascia

The soffit is the underside of the eaves and/or patio area connecting the exterior walls to the roof and is usually made of wood, vinyl or composite products such as Hardy Board. The fascia is the siding installed on the butt end of the rafters.

*Soffit & Fascia*

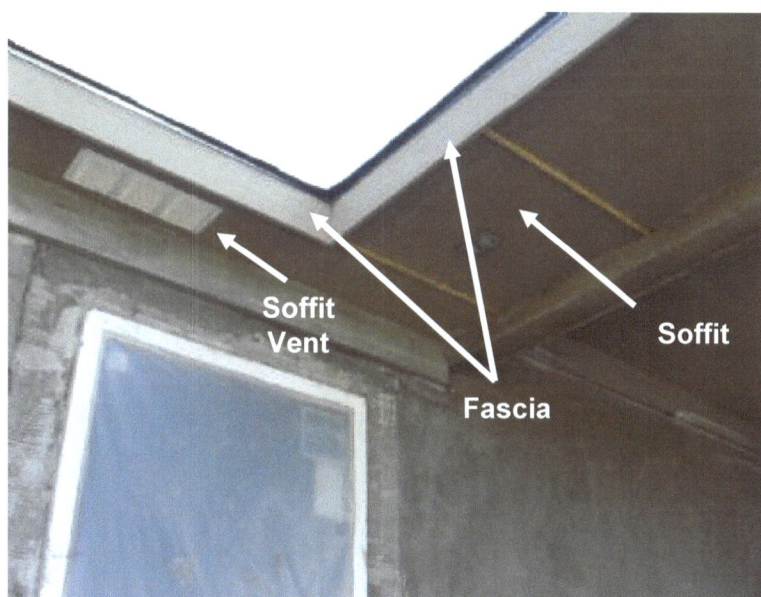

Soffit Vents provide ventilation in the attic to keep the attic cooler.

The fascia is usually made of 1"X4" or 1"X6" lumber or composite products

## Exterior Veneer

Exterior veneer/finish is the finish product put on the home to serve as a barrier from weather but has no structural support for the home and is mainly decorative.

### Siding

Exterior covering made of vinyl, aluminum, wood or composite materials such as Hardy Board installed to weatherproof the house.

*Wood Siding*

Wood siding can be planks or cedar shakes.

*Cedar Shakes*

*Vinyl Siding*

The picture on the left shows vinyl siding being installed on a home.

## Stucco

Exterior covering made of a durable, plaster-like substance installed to weatherproof the house. It includes the wire mesh, coating and sealer but not paint.

*Stucco*

Stucco has been applied in the picture on the left.

*Wire Mesh prior to application of stucco*

The wire mesh provides strength and durability to the stucco application.

## Masonry Veneer

Brick veneer on the exterior of a home provides weather protection but is not designed to support the weight of the structure.

*Brick Veneer*

The picture at the left depicts brick during installation.

*Stone Veneer*

Stone
Veneer

*Rock Veneer*

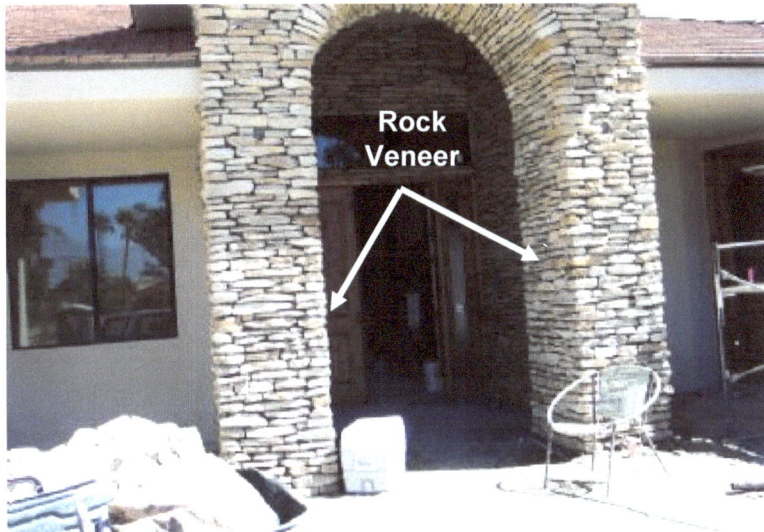

Rock
Veneer

## Exterior Trim

Exterior trim is all decorative work on the exterior of the house usually made of wood such as shutters or window trim.  It can also include masonry items such as columns or balustrades.

*Exterior Trim*

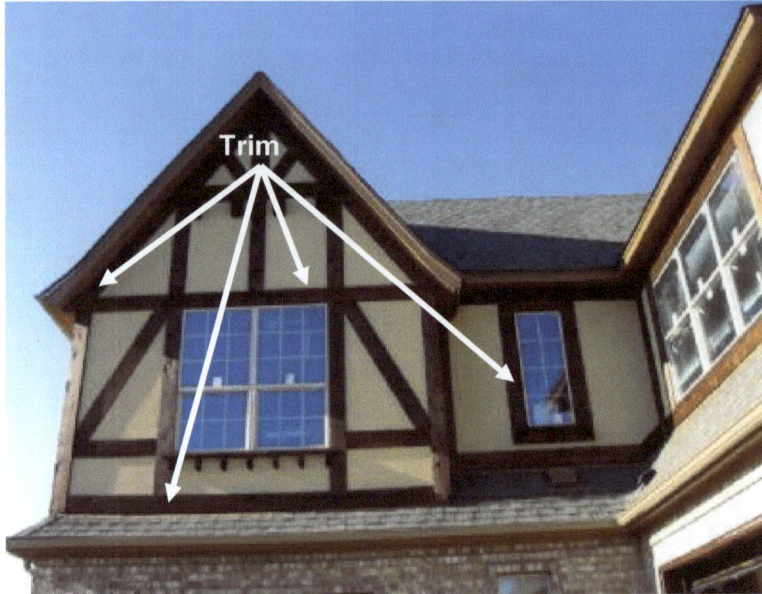

Exterior trim work originally intended as weatherproofing but today is primarily for decorative purposes.

*Exterior Trim Shutters*

Shutters and exterior window trimming are the most common types of exterior trim work.

*Balustrades to be installed*

*Balustrades after installation*

Balustrade

## Gutters/Downspouts

Metal or vinyl gutters are installed to carry water away from the structure.

*Gutters and Downspouts after installation*

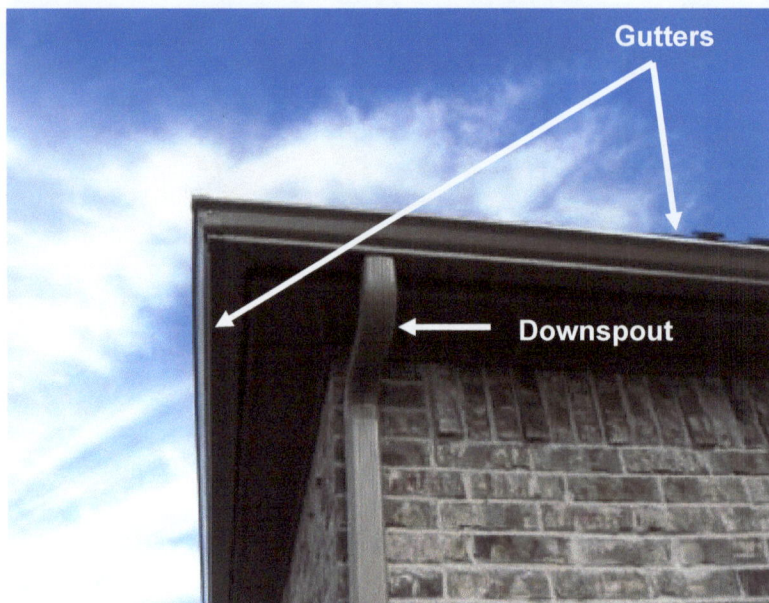

## Garage Doors

Garage doors include installation of garage doors, supports and openers.

*Garage Doors installed with Opener*

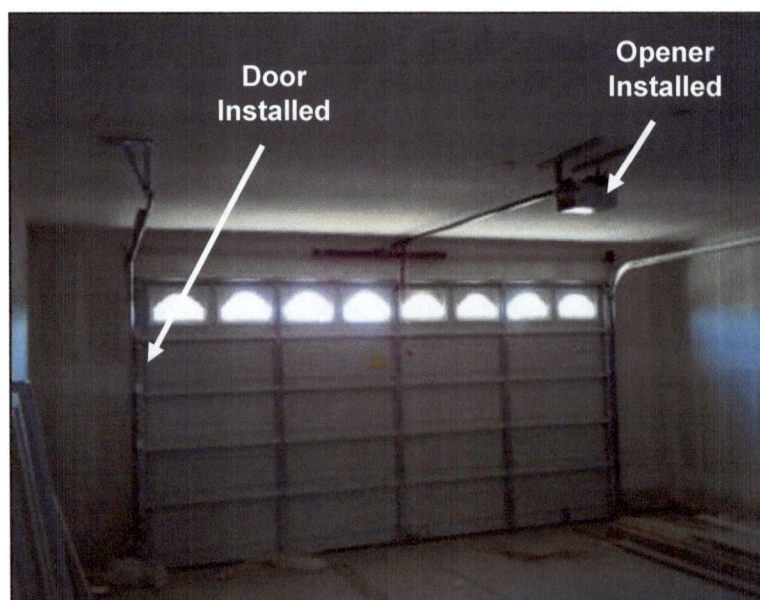

## Ornamental Iron

Ironwork inside or outside of house not designed to support any structural weight.

*Exterior Ornamental Iron Work*

*Interior Ornamental Iron Work*

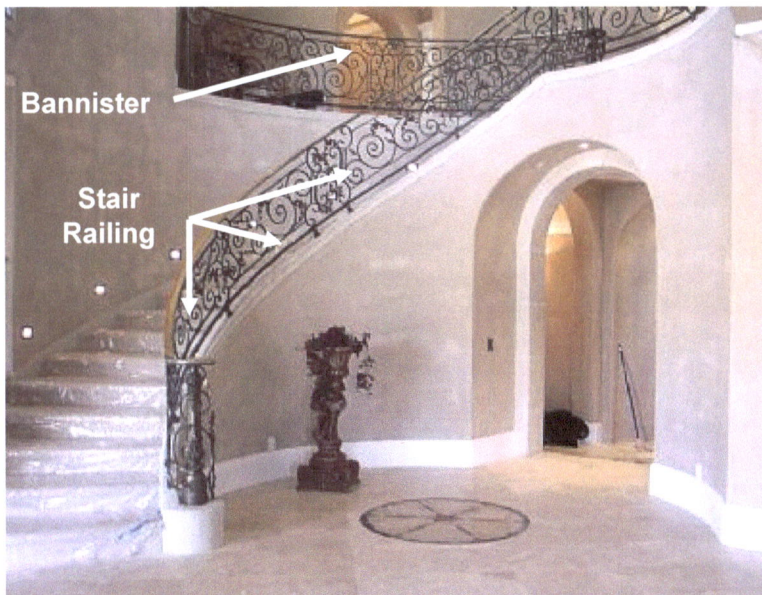

## Exterior Paint

Exterior painting is the latex or oil-base covering used primarily for weatherproofing but also decorative purposes.

*Painting*

**Review**

1. List the various types of roofs mentioned.

   _____

   _____

   _____

2. What are the most common veneer/finish items used?

   _____

   _____

   _____

3. A home has siding on one side only. What percent complete would you grant?

   _____%

4. Identify the three steps in the stucco application process.

   _____

   _____

   _____

5. What is the purpose of a Soffit Vent?

   _____

   _____

# Module #6
# Interior Finish

**Objectives** — After completing this module you will be able to:

☐  Identify the materials used to complete the finish out of the interior of the house.
☐  Understand the sequence in which certain steps must be completed.
☐  Estimate completion based on photo evidence.

## Definition

Interior Finish indicates the completion of all work inside the house and the interior is ready to paint and/or stain.

## Components of Interior Finish

- **Insulation:** Batting (generally fiberglass) used to retain heat or cooling and can be installed in strips (walls & ceiling) or blown in (attic).

- **Drywall (or Plaster):** Manufactured panel made out of gypsum plaster and encased in thin cardboard that is nailed or screwed onto the framing. The seams are taped and covered with a "joint compound."

- **Interior Stairs**: The risers, spindles and hand rails for the stairs. It may include the steps if they are not to be carpeted.

- **Cabinetry:** All interior cabinets and doors to be installed in the house.

- **Finish Materials & Millwork:** All wood and/or stone trim in the house for the trim work throughout the interior of the house. It can include base and crown moldings, coiffured ceilings and mantles.

- **Interior Doors:** All interior doors are installed and set in place.

## Insulation

Batting (generally fiberglass) used to retain heat or cooling and can be installed in strips (walls & ceiling) or blown in (attic).

*Rolled Insulation prior to installation*

Batten usually comes in rolls for easy installation.

*Rolled Batten Insulation installed in walls*

Insulation is the first activity to occur since the drywall is installed over the insulation and cabinets are installed over drywall.

*Blown Insulation prior to installation*

Blown insulation is usually packaged in bundles for easy storage and transportation.

*Blown Insulation in the attic*

Attic insulation is usually 12" - 18" thick.

## Foam Insulation

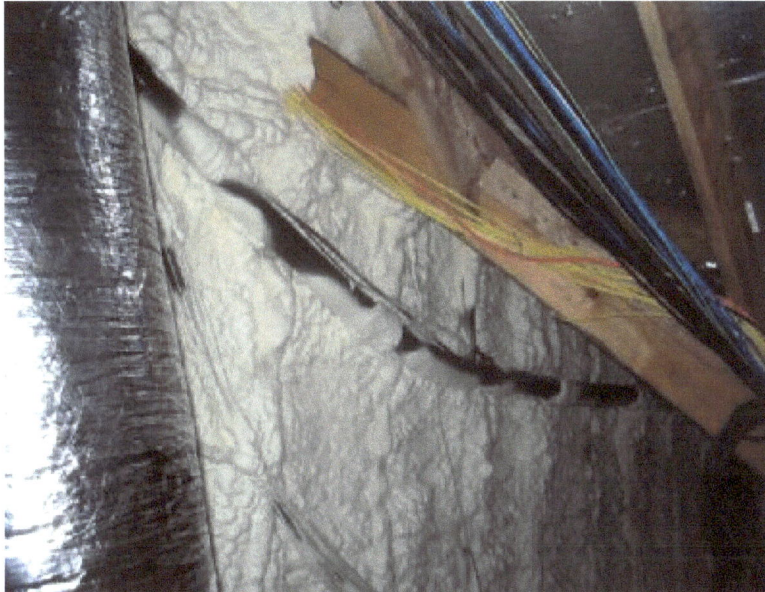

Foam insulation is usually sprayed in and expands to fill in gaps as it dries.

Usage of foam insulation has increased in recent years.

## Drywall

Drywall or sheetrock is a manufactured panel made out of gypsum plaster and encased in thin cardboard that is nailed or screwed onto the framing. The seams are taped and covered with a "joint compound."

*Drywall not completely taped and bedded*

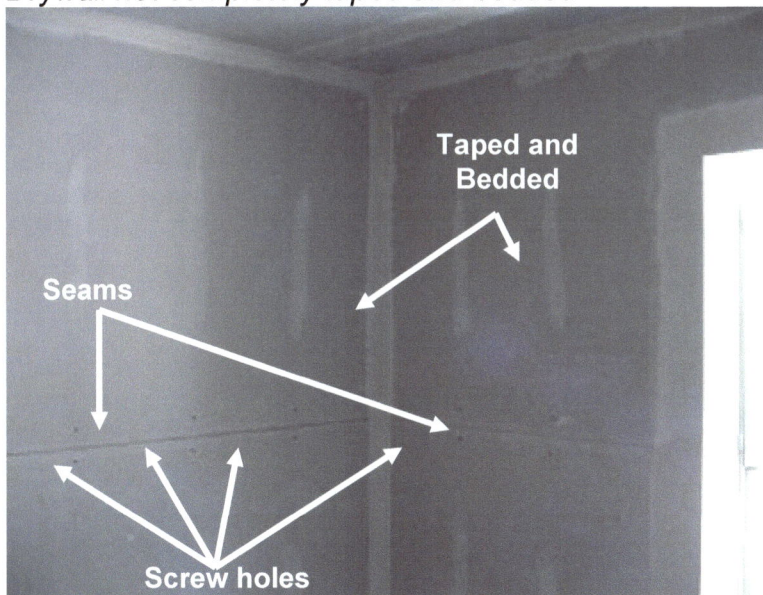

Drywall can be broken down into three primary components:
  ➢ Material
  ➢ Hanging
  ➢ Tape, Bed & Texturing

Drywall material usually comes in 4' X 8' or 4' X 12' sections.

## Drywall Taped and Bedded

Taped and Bedded

Drywall installed but not taped, bedded and textured would be considered 50% complete.

Texturing is primarily used to hide slight imperfections caused by small bubbles in the drywall "mud" or any variation in the straightness of the walls. Texturing is applied in most homes, but generally not in areas to be covered with wall paper.

## Cabinetry

Cabinetry includes all interior cabinets, drawers and doors to be installed in the house.

### Cabinets installed

The picture at the left shows cabinets 100% complete. The painting and staining are generally completed by a separate contractor.

## Finish Materials & Millwork (sometimes referred to as Interior Trim)

Finish Materials and Millwork includes all wood and/or stone trim throughout the interior of the house. It can include base and crown moldings, coiffured ceilings and mantles. Sometimes interior trim and doors are combined into the line item called "Interior Trim." The percent complete granted for this is typically divided between the elements included in the line item. For example, assume the doors are installed but the trim material is not installed. The percent complete would be estimated at 50%.

*Finish Millwork & Carpentry*

*Moldings*

## Interior Trim

The picture at the left indicates Interior Trim is complete. Note - the door would not be included in the "Interior Trim" line item since it is an Exterior or Entry Door.

## Interior Stairs

The risers, spindles and hand rails for the stairs. It may include the steps if they are not to be carpeted.

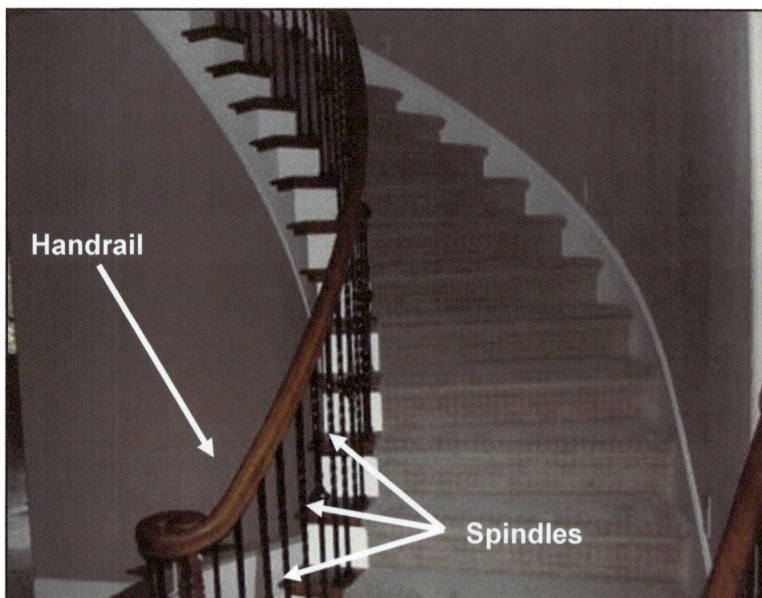

The picture at the left would still be considered 100% complete without the carpet installed. The stair contractor has completed all work and the carpet installer will be responsible for installing the carpet on the stairs.

## Interior Doors

All interior doors are installed and set in place.

*Onsite but not installed*

Most interior doors are delivered to the worksite already in the door jamb for easy installation.

**Review**

1. What are the different steps of drywall installation?

   _____

   _____

   _____

2. If the line item "Interior Trim" includes doors and only the interior doors are installed, but interior moldings, windows or doors trim are not installed, what percent complete should be granted for Interior Trim?_____%

3. In a home with 10 interior doors in which 3 are not installed, what percent should be given? _____%

4. What percent complete is given when the interior trim is installed but not painted or stained? _____%

5. Name the three most common types of insulation used in residential construction today.

   _____

   _____

   _____

# Module #7
# Finish Items

**Objectives** — After completing this module you will be able to:

☐ Identify the primary components involved in the finish out of a house
☐ Estimate completion based on photo evidence

## Definition

Finish Items means all items both inside and outside of a house have been completed to the home's specifications and the plans and specs appraisal.

## Components of Finish Items

- **Countertops:** All countertops in the kitchen, baths and/or other interior rooms in the house. Generally constructed of Formica, tile, wood or other solid surface materials like granite or soapstone.

- **Tub/Shower/Enclosures:** One-piece or component type tubs and showers installed in the house.

- **Interior Paint:** Painting or staining all walls, cabinets and trim within the house.

- **Hard Surface Finish Flooring:** All hard flooring including wood, marble, brick, vinyl and tile.

- **Carpeting:** The installation of both the carpet and the carpet pad.

- **Appliances:** The installation of all appliances usually in the kitchen and laundry rooms.

- **Finish Hardware:** All doorknobs, drawer pulls and other hardware inside the house.

- **Finish Plumbing:** All plumbing elements have been installed in the cabinets, tubs and showers, and are connected to the rough plumbing stub-outs.

- **Plumbing Fixtures:** The installation of all plumbing fixtures including faucets, shower heads and toilets.

- **Finish Electrical:** All electrical fixtures installed and permanent power is connected to the house.

- **Lighting Fixtures:** All plugs, switches, light fixtures, smoke detectors, appliances, bath ventilation fans installed. Some draw inspection forms include a separate line item for lighting fixtures.

- **Finish Heating, Ventilation, A/C:** Installation of vents, thermostat and exterior compressors.

- **Bath Accessories:** Towel racks and other bathroom accessories.

- **Tub and Shower Doors/Mirrors:** Shower doors and bathroom mirrors installed.

- **Finish Grading:** Distributing the soil around the house so that it directs water away from the structure; also ready for landscaping.

- **Pool/Spa:** Installation of pool and/or spa as a separate unit from the house.

- **Hardscape:** All driveway, sidewalks, porches, patios and/or steps outside the house.

- **Fencing including Gates:** Exterior fencing or walls separating the property from others and made of wood, metal or stone.

- **Landscaping:** Landscaping includes all trees, shrubs, grass sod or seed for the exterior of the house. Landscaping should prevent soil erosion. In addition, landscaping includes all decorative treatments including, but not limited to trees, shrubs, grass, rocks, stone pavers and walkways.

- **Central Vacuum:** Vacuum unit that includes piping in the wall, the central unit and all wall plates for attaching the hoses. The central unit is usually installed in a closet or the garage.

## Countertops

The line item "Countertops" includes all countertops in the kitchen, baths and/or other interior rooms. These are generally constructed of tile, Formica, wood or other solid surface materials like granite or soapstone.

*Tile Countertop*

Tile countertops also include the installation of the tile backsplash.

*Formica Countertop*

Formica countertops are usually cut onsite and glued in place.

*Granite Countertop*

When countertops are complete for one room but not another, approximate square footage is appropriate in determining the percent complete for the entire line item. For example, if kitchen countertops are installed but the bathroom countertops are not installed, and the kitchen accounts for 70% of the total square feet of countertop space, the percent complete should be 70%.

## Tub/Shower/Enclosures

One-piece or component type tubs and showers installed in the house.

*Bath/Shower enclosure*

## Interior Paint

Painting or staining all walls, cabinets and trim within the house.

*Painting*

Painting and staining for the two pictures on the left are both considered 100% complete.

*Staining*

## Hard Surface Finish Flooring

Hard surface flooring including wood, marble, brick, vinyl and tile.

*Hardwood Floor Installation*

When estimating the percent complete for a partially installed floor, use the approximate square footage that has been completed and divide into the total square feet to be installed.

For example, if there is 1,200 square feet to be installed in three rooms, and only 600 square feet are installed in one room and 300 square feet in another, the total completed is 900 square feet or 75%.

*Hardwood Flooring installed*

## Marble Flooring

Sometimes, brick, tile and even marble flooring will require a coat of sealant before it is finished. Whenever possible, ask the subcontractor if the floor tiles or bricks have been delivered already sealed by the manufacturer.

## Brick Flooring

## Vinyl Flooring

The vinyl flooring at the left would be considered approximately 50% installed since it is laid in place but not trimmed or glued down.

## Tile Flooring

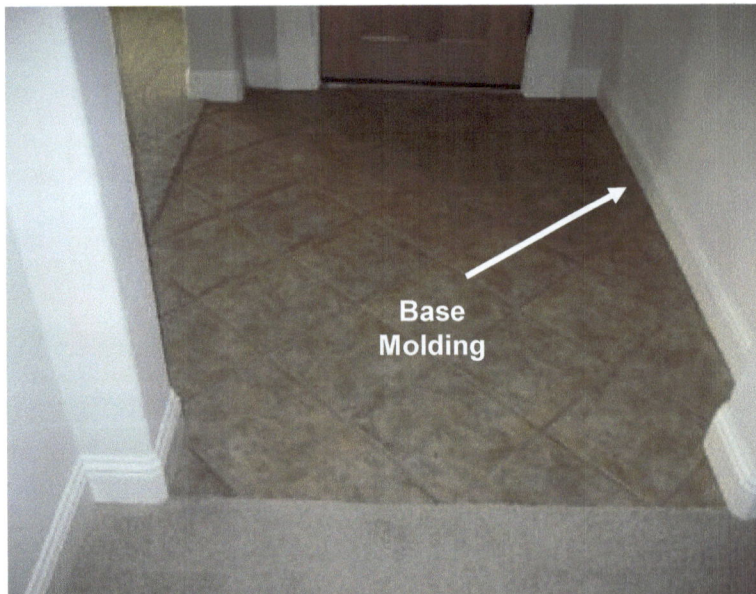

**Base Molding**

A visual cue that the tile on the left is 100% complete is the installation of the base molding which rests on top of the tile and can be used to cover any slight variations in the height of the tile.

## Carpeting

Carpeting includes the installation of both the carpet and the carpet pad.

*Carpet Installation*

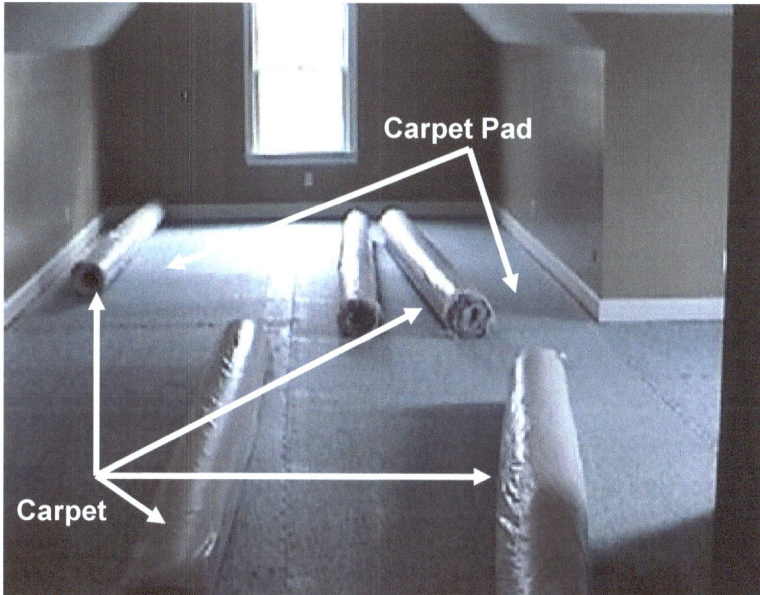

The photo on the left represents carpet installation at 50% complete.

*Carpet Installed*

A very good indication that the carpet is 100% complete is that temporary runners have been laid over to prevent the carpet from getting dirty from visitors walking on it.

## Appliances

Appliances include the installation of all appliances usually in the kitchen and laundry rooms.

*Appliances Ready to install*

Appliances are usually delivered to the worksite in one bulk drop.

*Appliances installed*

Appliances Installed

## Finish Hardware

Finish hardware means all doorknobs, drawer pulls and other hardware inside the house.

*Door Hardware*

Hardware is generally installed after all painting and staining have been completed.

*Cabinet Hardware*

## Finish Plumbing

All plumbing elements have been installed in the cabinets, tubs and showers, and connected to the rough plumbing stub-outs.

*Plumbing Finish*

The finish plumbing in both pictures on the left is 100% complete.

*Tub Installation*

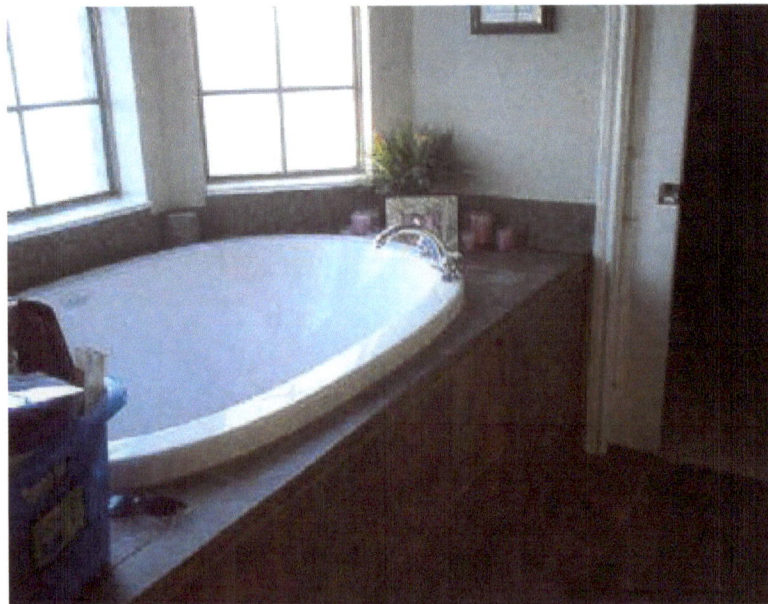

## Plumbing Fixtures

Plumbing fixtures include the installation of faucets, shower heads, sinks, toilets and usually includes the tub in the Master Bathroom.

*Faucets*

Plumbing fixtures are not considered 100% complete until water runs and completely drains from the fixture and the house.

*Shower Heads*

*Master Bathtub*

*Toilets*

## Finish Electrical

All electrical fixtures installed and permanent power is connected to the house.

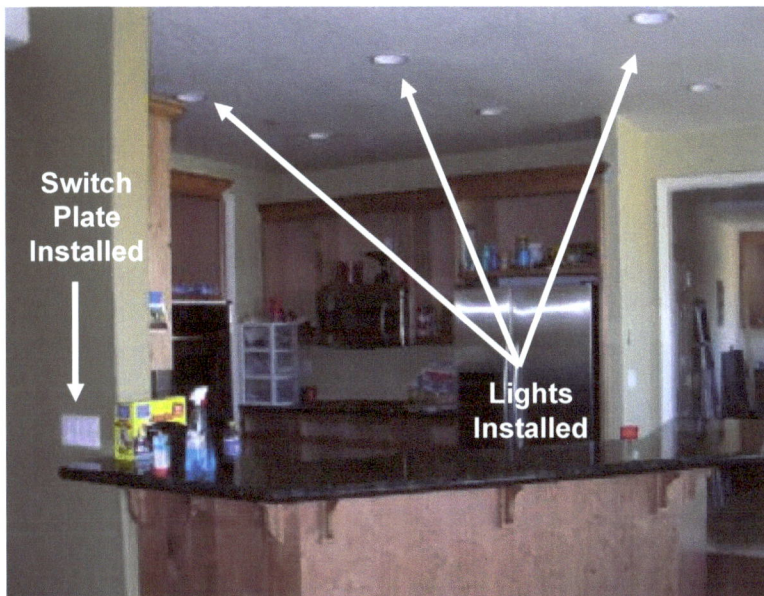

Finish Electric is not considered 100% complete until the fixtures and electrical appliances are fully functional.

## Lighting Fixtures

All plugs, switches, light fixtures, smoke detectors, appliances and bath ventilation fans installed. Some draw inspection forms include a separate line item for lighting fixtures.

If the draw inspection form has a separate line item for Lighting Fixtures from Finish Electric, then the fixtures can be granted 100% complete upon installation even if the power is not connected and they cannot produce light.

## Finish Heating, Ventilation, A/C

Installation of vents, thermostat and exterior compressors

*Thermostat*

The thermostat is generally the last interior item installed so it usually means the interior portion of the Finish HVAC is complete.

*HVAC Vent*

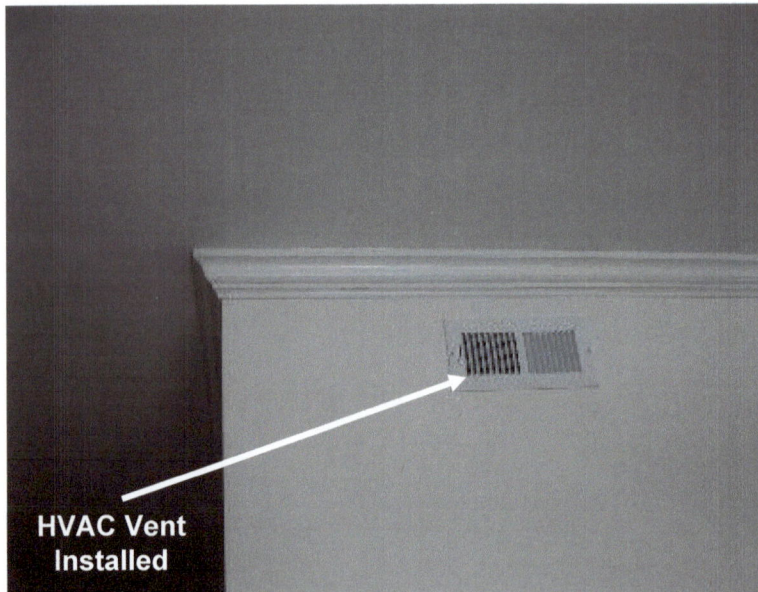

**HVAC Vent Installed**

*Compressor*

Finish HVAC is not considered 100% complete until the compressors and thermostat are installed.

## Bath Accessories

Bath accessories include towel racks, soap dishes and other bathroom accessories.

*Bath Accessories*

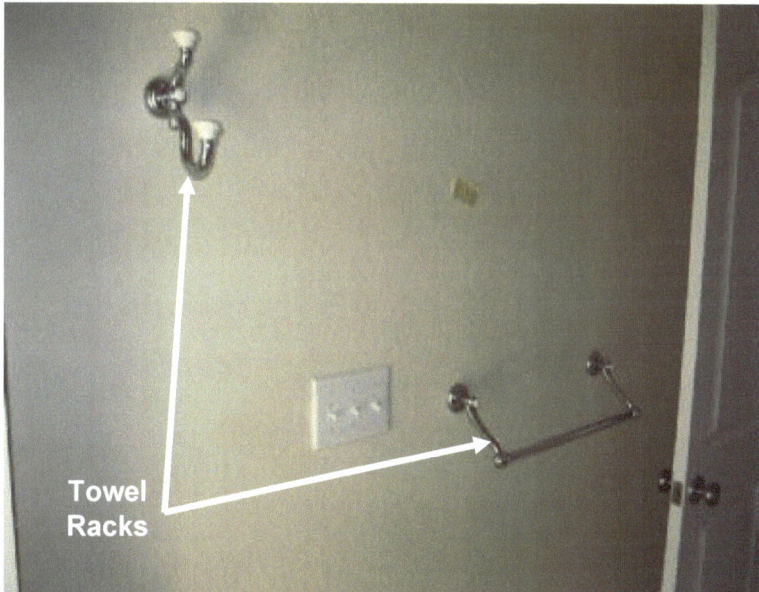

Towel Racks

## Tub and Shower Doors/Mirrors

Shower doors and bathroom mirrors are installed.

*Bath Mirrors*

*Shower Doors*

## Finish Grading

Finish grading is the distribution of the soil around the house so that it directs water away from the structure; also ready for landscaping.

*Graded Away from House*

Finish Grading is usually completed prior to the installation of the irrigation or sprinkler system.

## Pool/Spa

Pool and Spa include the installation of pool and/or spa as a separate unit from the house.

*Pool*

*Spa*

*Pool/Spa Equipment*

## Hardscape

Hardscaping includes all driveways, sidewalks, porches, patios and/or steps outside the house.

*Driveway*

Hardscaping is sometimes referred to as Flatwork.

*Walkways and Patios*

---

## Fencing including Gates

Fencing includes exterior fencing or walls separating the property from others and is made of wood, metal or stone.

*Fencing*

*Gates*

## Landscaping

Landscaping includes all trees, shrubs, grass sod or seed for the exterior of the house. Landscaping should prevent soil erosion. In addition, landscaping includes all decorative treatments including but not limited to trees, shrubs, grass, rocks, stone pavers and walkways.

## Central Vacuum

The central vacuum includes the piping in the wall, the central unit and all wall plates for attaching the hoses. The central unit is usually installed in a closet, the basement, or the garage.

*Central Vacuum Central Unit*

## Review

1. Name the three most common elements found in Hardscaping.

   _____

   _____

   _____

2. Hard Surface Finish Flooring includes all of the following except:
   - ☐ Wood flooring
   - ☐ Carpeting
   - ☐ Tile
   - ☐ Vinyl
   - ☐ Marble

3. Finish Plumbing includes the installation of all sinks, fixtures, tubs and toilets to the point where water will drain from the house.  T / F

4. What is the purpose of Finish Grading?

   _____

   _____

5. What items must be complete to report Finish HVAC at 100%?
   - ☐ Compressor
   - ☐ Thermostat
   - ☐ Interior Vent Covers
   - ☐ Air Filters
   - ☐ Insulation

# Module #8
## Draw Form

**Objectives** – After completing this module, you will be able to:

☐ Identify a Draw Inspection form correctly
☐ Recognize the differences between Draw Inspection Form types
☐ Understand the different components of a Draw Inspection form

### Understanding Various Types of Draw Inspection Forms:

The Line Item form referenced below is an example to explain what components a draw form will typically contain. There are multiple options of forms that an inspector may come upon depending on the bank/lender, but this form tends to be one of the most highly used.

Draw Inspection Form Variations:

- **Line Item**: List of individual construction items and the dollar amount each represents of the total amount of funds.

- **Fixed Percent**: List of individual construction items and the different percentage of the total amount of funds each represents.

- **Stage/Phase**: The construction items are broken down into stages/phases and funds are assigned to each stage/phase. Once the construction for the stage/phase is completed, the funds will be released from the lender.

- **AIA (American Institute of Architects) Draw Request**: Created by architects for commercial use and adopted by residential. Similar to a Line Item report, but credit is only given for the line items and the amounts requested by the builder/developer. If a job is 100 percent done but the builder only requested 50 percent then that is the amount they will receive no matter the completion.

### General Components of a Draw Inspection Form:

- **Header**: Contains information about the property and the builder. It also contains specific details pertaining to the inspection itself (e.g. date ordered, date to inspect). The Header acts as an identifier for a specific draw inspection.

- **Line Item Number (#)**: Allows for easy reference to line item descriptions. It works as an identifier and normally will follow in a sequential order unless customizations have been provided by the lender.

- **Item Description**: States what part of the construction project the specific line is referring to by giving a brief explanation of the task.

- **Amount**: The total amount of funds allotted for a line item.

- **Prior Inspection**: The percent in this column indicates how much of the project had been completed at the time of the previous inspection.

- **Funded**: A dollar amount stating how much of the funds the builder has already received in relation to the percentage previously completed.

- **This Inspection**: A percentage determined by the inspector for each item informing lenders of the amount of construction completed after inspection.

- **Eligible to Fund**: An amount based on the overall progress of the construction project.

- **Inspector's Remarks**: Comments made by the inspector giving a more in-depth update on the completion progress.

- **Photo Section**: Photos attached to the report illustrate the work in the written report.

*Header*

## TRINITY INSPECTION SERVICES, LLC - DRAW INSPECTION RESULTS
## 1-888-573-8029

Lender Information →

| PROPERTY INFORMATION | BUILDER INFORMATION |
|---|---|
| **Lender :** Test Bank of Trinity | **Builder :** ABC Contractor |
| **Loan / Draw # :** Draw-123MainStreet / 1 | **Builder Contact :** John Smith |
| **Borrower :** Harris, Sarah | **Builder Phone :** 555-555-5555  **Cell :** |
| **Address :** 123 Main Street | **County :** Dallas |
| Anywhere, TX 75001 | **Date Ordered :** 4/5/2010 10:58:00 AM |
| **Phone : W: 555-555-5555 | H: 555-555-5555 | C: |** | **Date to Inspect :** 4/5/2010 10:58:00 AM |
| **Ordered By : Shanda Customer** | **Date Inspected :** 4/2/2010 **Status:** Report Completed - Revised |
| **Inspected By :** 21392 SV | **Date Completed :** 4/6/2010 4:17:12 PM |
| | **Invoice # :** 10-351093 |

← Builder Information

Borrower Information

Inspection Information

*Remaining Sections*

Line Item Number (#)   Item Description   Amount  Prior Inspection  This Inspection

| # | Item Description | Amount | Prior Inspection | Funded | This Inspection | Eligible to Fund |
|---|---|---|---|---|---|---|
| 02.01 | Administrative & Indirect costs of construction | $5,000.00 | 0% | $0.00 | 0% | $0.00 |
| **** | **Inspector's remarks:** Rolls in overall cost of construction. | | | | | |

Inspector's Remarks

Funded       Eligible to Fund

# Report Line Items

The example below exemplifies how the modules mentioned previously work together to complete a draw inspection. "Cabinets" fall under the interior Finish module, while "Doors – Garage & Openers" fits neatly into the Exterior Weather Tight module.

An interesting note to make is "Doors – Interior/Exterior" finds itself falling into two categories because Interior doors are in the Interior Finish module and Exterior doors are in the Exterior Weather Proof module.

On this report, the reader will notice the "This Inspection" column has a completion percent assigned to it and that is reflected in the "Eligible to Fund" column.

## Report Line Items

| # | Item Description | Amount | Prior Inspection | Funded | This Inspection | Eligible to Fund |
|---|---|---|---|---|---|---|
| 02.22 | Cabinets | $15,000.00 | 0% | $0.00 | 0% | $0.00 |
| 02.23 | Doors - Interior/Exterior | $10,000.00 | 0% | $0.00 | 25% | $2,500.00 |
| **** | Inspector's remarks: 7 doors are on back order. | | | | | |
| 02.24 | Doors - Garage & Openers | $7,000.00 | 0% | $0.00 | 80% | $5,600.00 |
| **** | Inspector's remarks: Garage door openers need to be ordered and set up with a code. | | | | | |
| 02.25 | Staircase/Railings | $16,000.00 | 0% | $0.00 | 95% | $15,200.00 |
| **** | Inspector's remarks: Railing is not installed. | | | | | |
| 02.26 | Rough Plumbing | $30,000.00 | 0% | $0.00 | 100% | $30,000.00 |

Soft costs will also be found in the report line items. Pictured below are some examples of soft costs. Both "Clean Up" and "Rough Carpentry Labor" are items that cannot be pictured but are still a part of the construction costs. As a reminder, hard costs are the costs that can be pictured.

## Soft Costs

| # | Item Description | Amount | Prior Inspection | Funded | This Inspection | Eligible to Fund |
|---|---|---|---|---|---|---|
| 02.09 | Clean Up | $4,000.00 | 0% | $0.00 | 0% | $0.00 |
| 02.17 | Rough Carpentry Labor | $5,000.00 | 0% | $0.00 | 100% | $5,000.00 |

## Photo Section

Photographs give evidence to what the inspector stated in the written report. The photos above have labels that describe what each picture portrays.

*Photos*

SECURITY SYSTEM

LIVING ROOM WITH FIREPLACE / FLUE

DOORS - EXTERIOR

LIVING ROOM WITH WINDOWS

**Review**

1. What are the different draw inspection form variations?

   _____

   _____

   _____

2. Which form variation is most commonly used?

   _____

3. What information goes in the form's header?

   _____

   _____

4. What purpose does the photo section serve?

   _____

   _____

   _____

# Review Answer Key

## Module 2: Site Preparation

1. Photos of property, addresses posted on the property of the house, permits identifying the property and meet the owner/builder at the property
2. Mowing of the grass and weeds, the removal of large rocks and the trimming and removal of trees and shrubs
3. Rough Grading
4. Temporary Barriers

## Module 3: Foundation

1. Pier and Beam, Basement and Concrete Slab
2. Piers: Depth stabilization/support & Footers: Support pads/base
3. Rebar Slab and Post-Tension Slab
4. Begin at the bottom of foundation and run to approximately 6" above the ground line for best protection

## Module 4: Building Rough-In

1. Plumbing Top-out, Rough HVAC, Rough Electrical, Fire Protection, Security and Communications Pre-Wire
2. Attic, Basement
3. No, occurs during Finish Electrical
4. False
5. Wood, Concrete, Steel
6. 0%

## Module 5: Exterior Weather-Tight

1. Shingled Roof, Title Roof, Tin Roof
2. Siding, Stucco, Masonry Veneer
3. 25%
4. Wire Mesh Application, Coating, Sealer
5. Provide ventilation in the attic to keep the attic cooler

## Module 6: Interior Finish

1. Material is installed and then taped, bedded and/or texture is added
2. 50%
3. 70%
4. 100%
5. Rolled Batten, Blown Insulation, Foam Insulation

## Module 7: Finish Items

1. Driveways, Walkways, Patios
2. Carpeting
3. True
4. Distributing soil around the house so that it directs water away from the structure and prepares soil for landscaping.
5. Compressors, Thermostat, Interior Vent Covers

## Module 8: Draw Form

1. Line Item, Fixed Percent, Stage/Phase, AIA Draw Request
2. Line Item Form
3. Lender Information, Borrower Information, Builder Information, Inspection Information
4. Give evidence of the information in the written portion

# Index

## A

AIA Draw Request, 98
Air Duct, *See* HVAC Duct
Amount, 1, 2, 4, 98, 99, 100
Appliances, 73, 74, 82, 87

## B

Balusters, *See* Balustrade
Balustrade, 58, 59
Basement, 1, 17, 19, 20, 22, 29, 36, 37, 96
Bath Accessories, 74, 89
Batt, *See* Batten
Batten, 64, 65
Beam, 17, 20, 21, 28
Bearing, 17, 20, 26, 28, 34, 45
Blown Insulation, 64, 65, 66
Brick Veneer, 46, 56
Building Rough-In, 3, 26

## C

Cabinetry, 64, 68, 100
Carpeting, 73, 81, 97
Central Vacuum, 74, 96
Clearing, 4, 7, 8, 16
Concrete Slab, 17, 20, 23
Contractor, 2, 21, 68, 70
Countertops, 73, 75
Crawl Space, 20

## D

Demolition, 4, 6
Domestic Water Well, 4, 14
Doors, 45, 46, 51, 52, 60, 64, 68, 69, 71, 72, 74, 90, 101
Draw Inspection, 1, 2, 12, 98, 101
Drywall, 39, 64, 67, 68, 72
Duct, *See* HVAC Duct

## E

Eaves, 45, 53
Eligible to Fund, 99, 101
Embedded Hardware, 17, 18
Enclosures, 73, 76
Excavation, 4, 9

## Exterior

Exterior Doors, 51, 101
Exterior Paint, 46, 62
Exterior Trim, 46, 58
Exterior Veneer, 46, 54
Exterior Weather-Tight, 3, 45

## F

Fascia, 45, 53
Fencing, 74, 94
Fill-Type Insulation, *See* Blown Insulation
Finish Electrical, 73, 87
Finish Grading, 13, 74, 91, 97
Finish Hardware, 73, 83
Finish Heating, Ventilation, A/C, 74, 88
Finish Items, 3, 63, 73
Finish Materials, 64, 69
Finish Plumbing, 73, 84, 97
Fire Protection, 27, 40
Fireplace, 41
Fixed Percent Form, 98
Flatwork, 93
Floor Decking, 29, 32
Flue, 41
Foundation, 2, 3, 17, 18, 19, 20, 23, 24, 25, 36, 44, 45
Funded, 99, 100

## G

Garage Doors, 46, 60, 101
Gates, 74, 94
Glazing, 45, 53
Grading, 4, 9, 10, 74, 91, 97
Ground Electrical, 20
Ground Mechanical, 19
Ground Plumbing, 19
Ground Utilities, 19
Ground Utilities/Mechanicals, 17
Gutters/Downspouts, 46, 60

## H

Hard Costs, 2, 101
Hard Surface Finish Flooring, 73, 78, 97
Hardscape, 74, 93
Hardwood, 78
Header, 99, 100
Hips, 47
Home Construction, 1, 3

## I

Inspector's Remarks, 98, 100
Insulation, 39, 64, 65, 66, 67, 72, 97

Interior Doors, 64, 71, 72, 101
Interior Finish, 3, 64, 101
Interior Paint, 73, 77
Interior Partitions, 26, 32
Interior Stairs, 44, 64, 70
Interior Trim, 69, 70, 72
Item Description, 99, 100

## J

Jamb, 71
Joist, 20, 30

## K

## L

Landscaping, 74, 91, 95
Lighting Fixtures, 74, 87
Lightweight Concrete Interior, 26, 35
Line Item Form, 98
Line Item Number, 98, 100
Load Bearing, 26, 28

## M

Manufactured Trusses / Components, 26, 33
Masonry Veneer, 46, 56
Millwork, 64, 69
Mirrors, 74, 90
Modular / Prefabricated Housing, 2, 26, 27, 42
Moisture Barrier, 31, 45, 47
Molding, 64, 69, 72, 80

## N

## O

Ornamental Iron, 46, 61

## P

Permits, 2, 5, 6
Photo Section, 99, 102
Pier and Beam, 20
Plasterboard, *See* Drywall
Plates, 39, 44, 74, 96
Plumbing Fixtures, 73, 84, 85
Plumbing Top-out, 26, 36
Pool, 74, 91, 92
Post Tension Slab, 23
Prior Inspection, 99, 100
Private Septic System, 4, 12

Pump House and Pressure water, 4, 15

## Q

## R

Radiant Heat, 38
Rafter, 30, 32, 33, 35, 45, 53
Reinforced Concrete, *See* Concrete Slab
Retaining Walls, 4, 11, 17, 24
Riser, 64, 70
Rock Work, 7, 46
Roof Covering, 45, 47
Roof Decking, 30, 34, 35
Roof Felt, 45, 47
Rough Electrical, 39, 44
Rough Framing, 26, 28, 30, 31, 44
Rough Grading, 4, 9, 10
Rough HVAC, 26, 37
Rough Mechanicals, 26, 36, 44
Rough Plumbing, 26, 36, 73, 84

## S

Sash, 45, 53
Security & Communications Pre-Wire, 27, 41
Septic Tank, 1, 13
Shakes, 54
Sheathing, 26, 30, 31, 34, 35
Shingles, 35, 45, 47, 49
Shower, 45, 49, 73, 74, 76, 84, 85, 90
Shower Doors, 74, 90
Siding, 45, 46, 53, 54, 55, 63
Site Preparation, 3, 4, 17, 45, 64, 73
Site Verification, 4, 5
Skylights, 45, 52
Slab, 17, 19, 20, 23, 25
Soffit, 45, 53, 63
Soft Costs, 2, 101
Spa, 74, 91, 92
Stacking, 43
Stage Form, 98
Stakeout, 4, 8
Structural Masonry, 26, 28, 30
Structural Steel, 21, 26, 29
Stucco, 45, 54, 62
Studs, 30, 31
Subcontractor, 32, 79

## T

Temporary Barrier, 4, 10
This Inspection, 99, 100, 101

Tie Beams, 28
Tie-Down Bolts, 17, 18
Tub, 36, 73, 74, 76, 84, 85, 86, 90, 97

# U

Underground Plumbing, 19

# V

Valley, 47

# W

Waterproofing, 45, 49
Weatherproofing, 17, 24, 46, 58, 62
Windows, 45, 50, 52, 53

# X

# Y

# Z

# Notes

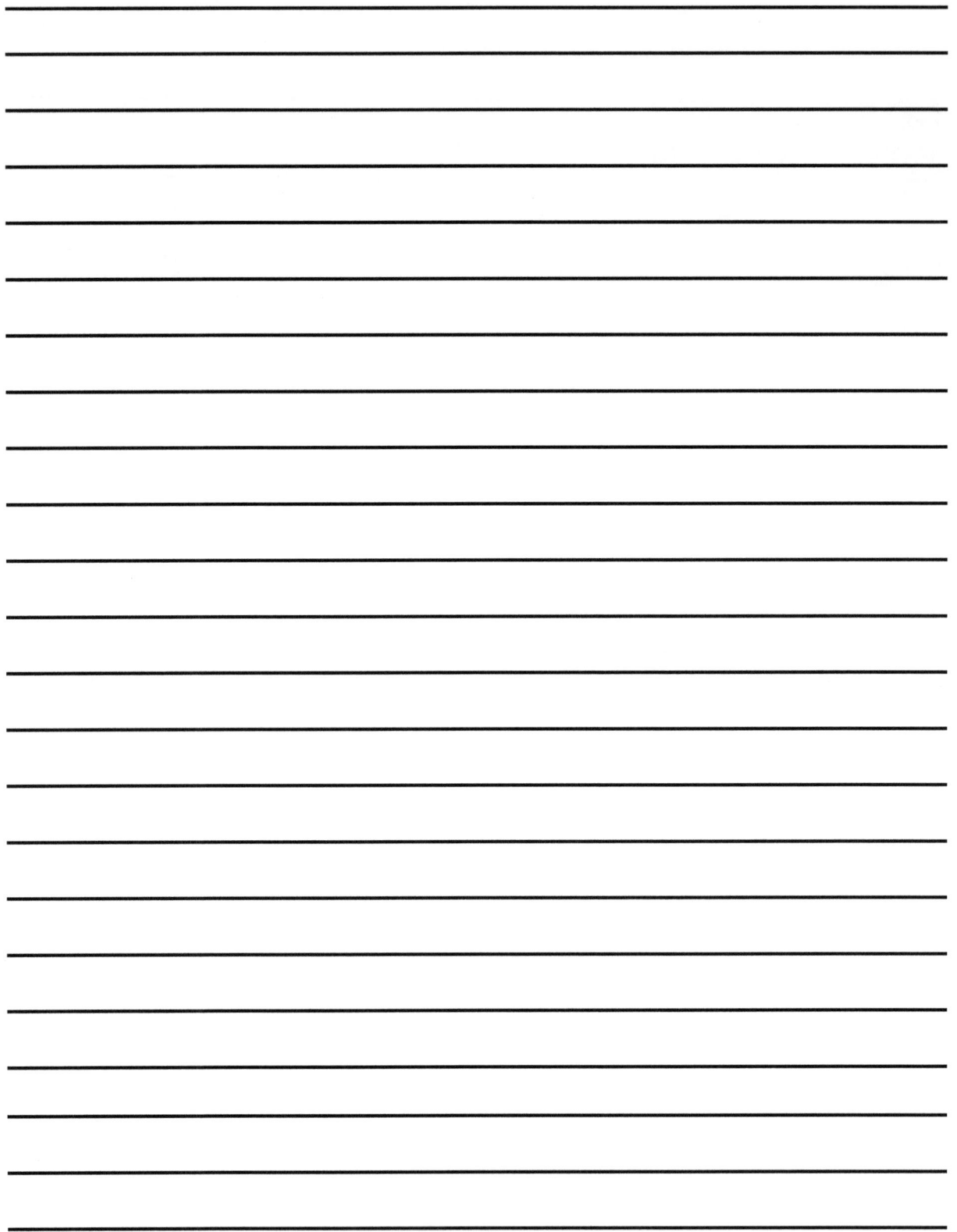

www.ingramcontent.com/pod-product-compliance
Lightning Source LLC
Chambersburg PA
CBHW041717210326
41598CB00007B/684